T0244774

THE SECRET TO ATTRACTING

About the Author

Richard Webster was born and raised in New Zealand. He has been interested in the psychic world since he was nine years old. As a teenager, he became involved in hypnotism and later became a professional stage hypnotist. After school, he worked in the publishing business and purchased a bookstore. The concept of reincarnation played a significant role in his decision to become a past-life specialist. Richard has also taught psychic development classes, which are based on many of his books.

Richard's first book was published in 1972, fulfilling a childhood dream of becoming an author. Richard is now the author of over a hundred books, and is still writing today. His bestselling books include *Spirit Guides & Angel Guardians* and *Creative Visualization for Beginners*.

Richard has appeared on several radio and TV programs in the United States and abroad. He currently resides in New Zealand with his wife and three children. He regularly travels the world to give lectures, hold workshops, and continue his research.

The Secret to Attracting
L·U·C·K

50 Ways
to
Manifest
Abundance
&
Good
Fortune

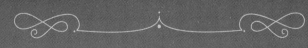

RICHARD WEBSTER

Llewellyn Publications
Woodbury, Minnesota

FIRST EDITION
First Printing, 2021

Cover design: Shannon McKuhen
Deluxe Silver Spiral Pendulum and Premium Amethyst Chakra Pendulum used with permission by Lo Scarabeo
Llewellyn Publications is a registered trademark of Llewellyn Worldwide Ltd.

Library of Congress Cataloging-in-Publication Data
Names: Webster, Richard, author.
Title: The secret to attracting luck : 50 ways to manifest abundance & good fortune / Richard Webster.
Description: First edition. | Woodbury, Minnesota : Llewellyn Publications, [2021] | Includes bibliographical references. | Summary: "A book of assorted pointers for increasing one's personal luck"—Provided by publisher.
Identifiers: LCCN 2020052581 (print) | LCCN 2020052582 (ebook) | ISBN 9780738766614 (paperback) | ISBN 9780738767000 (ebook)
Subjects: LCSH: Fortune. | Success.
Classification: LCC BF1778 .W433 2021 (print) | LCC BF1778 (ebook) | DDC 131-–dc23
LC record available at https://lccn.loc.gov/2020052581
LC ebook record available at https://lccn.loc.gov/2020052582

Llewellyn Publications
A Division of Llewellyn Worldwide Ltd.
2143 Woodale Drive
Woodbury, MN 55125-2989
www.llewellyn.com
Printed in the United States of America

Other Books by Richard Webster

Potential in the Palm of Your Hand
How to Use a Crystal
How to Use a Pendulum
Llewellyn's Complete Book of Divination
Playing Card Divination for Beginners
Tarot for Everyone Kit
Mind Reading Quick & Easy
Palm Reading for Beginners
You Can Read Palms
Practical Guide to Past-Life Memories
Is Your Pet Psychic?
The Complete Book of Palmistry
Seven Secrets to Success

For my lifelong friend, Robyn Berry Luke. The luckiest day in my life was when I met Margaret, my wife. That meeting was entirely due to you, and for that I'm eternally grateful.

CONTENTS

INTRODUCTION

The origin of the word "luck" is disputed, but one potential source was from the old Anglo-Saxon *âlæccan*, "to catch." Some fortunate people manage to catch good luck at birth and are described as having been born lucky. For most people, though, luck appears to be an intangible, capricious force that offers favor for a while and then disappears for no apparent reason. Luck is thus usually said to be something that happens by coincidence, accident, or chance. That might be true, but it defines only part of what luck actually is.

The Random House Dictionary defines luck as "the force that seems to operate for good or ill in a person's life, as in shaping circumstances, events, opportunities, etc." This definition is a highly positive one, as it shows that the most important factor in luck is you. You have the ability to use your own energy, or force, to shape your "circumstances, events, opportunities, etc." to create your own good luck.

1

People have always tried to improve their luck. The ancient Romans prayed to the goddess Fortuna, who was usually pictured holding a cornucopia from which she showered luck on those who worshiped her. Our modern term "Lady Luck" refers to Fortuna. The Greek goddess Tyche provided good fortune and luck to her followers. The Hindu goddess Lakshmi provides beauty as well as good luck. There are many other examples of gods and goddesses who could be called upon to help improve luck. Throughout history, people have used omens, portents, lucky charms, and a variety of other methods to help them improve their lot in life.

Everyone has experienced good luck of one sort or another. Averting or surviving a bad accident, meeting someone who became a life partner, or securing the perfect job are all examples.

Many people today claim there is no such thing as luck, yet millions of people regularly buy lottery tickets despite knowing how slim the odds are of winning. Winning a lottery is a matter of chance rather than luck; the results are entirely out of our hands.

We can't do anything about chance, but we can increase our luck dramatically by focusing on the things we can control. These include positive energy, the law of attraction, and the power of intention.

Positive energy is much more than thinking happy thoughts; it's an attitude or mindset that focuses on worthwhile, successful outcomes. People with positive energy know that even though life has both ups and downs, everything will work out in the long run.

The law of attraction says that you attract into your life anything that you focus on. The first step is to know what you want. Once you've decided on a goal and constantly feed it with positive energy, you'll ultimately reap positive rewards. As this law is impartial and works on what your mind focuses on, it's important to constantly think thoughts of happiness, abundance, and good luck. These thoughts go out into the universe and attract to you whatever it is you are focusing on.

The word "intention" has achieved great popularity in recent years. Intention is the starting point of any achievement. You must know what you want to accomplish before you start anything. When people know what they want, visualize themselves achieving it, focus intently on this goal, and work toward achieving it, the chances are high that they'll succeed. When they do, people who fail to do this consider them lucky.

The purpose of this book is to help you use the skills and abilities you already possess, or can develop, to create good luck in your life.

1

◆

ATTITUDE

The term "attitude" refers to a person's state of mind and often reveals how one thinks and acts. A positive attitude is a mental and emotional approach to life that expects positive results. Not surprisingly, it's one of the key ingredients for success. People with a positive attitude expect the best, while people with a negative attitude have a more pessimistic outlook and expect failure. As we all reap what we sow, both groups usually receive what they expect. When you approach people with a cheerful, friendly attitude, you're likely to receive the same response in return. Positive people live happy lives, while pessimistic and negative people are constantly frustrated with the adverse results they experience.

Fortunately, you have total control over your attitude, and turning a negative attitude into a positive one can transform your life. The American philosopher and psychologist

William James (1842–1910) said: "It is our attitude at the beginning of a difficult task which, more than anything else, will affect its successful outcome" (James, 80). Developing and maintaining a positive attitude has many benefits. You'll have an optimistic outlook on life, which will in turn eliminate most of the minor, everyday stresses and worries. You'll gain enough motivation and energy to achieve your goals. You'll believe in yourself and will be able to inspire others as well as yourself. You'll be willing to experiment and try things out without being concerned about failure. You'll be more productive in everything you do. You'll also handle stress much more easily.

Everything you do is affected by your attitude, even things as simple as going on a blind date. If you expect the date to be disastrous, that's what's likely to happen. Conversely, if you expect to have an enjoyable night out, you're likely to have a wonderful time. Two completely different possibilities determined largely by your attitude.

A positive attitude makes your days more pleasant, as you'll attract people who appreciate your positive approach. You'll meet more people, and be offered more opportunities as a result. Your attitude is entirely up to you. Consequently, it's also a vital factor in becoming lucky. Once you start considering yourself lucky, you'll find lucky experiences occurring on a regular basis.

To achieve good luck in life, you need to deliberately choose to have a positive attitude. Of course, everyone experiences bad days from time to time. When these occur, you might need to remind yourself to maintain a positive attitude. Most people pay little or no attention to their attitude at any given moment. Fortunately, you can change your attitude, and transform your life as a result. Here are some techniques that will help:

1. Find someone who already has the type of attitude you'd like to have, and model yourself on that person. They don't necessarily need to know what you're doing. However, if you can, spend time with this person and ask him or her questions about the benefits of having a positive attitude.

2. Spend time with positive people. Positive people help you maintain a good attitude, even when matters are not going well in your life. They'll lift you up and ensure that you look on the bright side of life rather than the negative. You can't expect to maintain a positive attitude if you spend much of your time with people who have a negative outlook on life.

3. Laugh frequently. It's impossible to feel downhearted when you're laughing. It's also important to learn how to laugh at yourself. We all take ourselves too seriously at times.

4. Respond positively. It's impossible to control everything, and situations that are out of our control occur frequently. In such situations, the only thing you can control is your attitude. Resolve to act positively, no matter what happens.

5. Help others. Volunteering your time and skills to help others makes them feel good, and this in turn raises your self-esteem and attitude.

6. Evaluate your attitude. Ask yourself if your current attitude is enabling you to live a happy, positive life, and have good relationships with others. If it isn't, think about one small thing you could do to improve your attitude. Focus on that until you've achieved it and then ask yourself the question again. Continue doing this until a positive attitude is a natural and permanent part of your life.

7. Observe your thoughts and speech. Whenever you find yourself expressing negative thoughts or opinions, pause and deliberately turn them around and make them positive.

8. Think about a time when you had a good attitude and recall the good energy you received as a result. Recall how much smoother and easier life was when you were in that state. You can recapture all of the positive aspects of having a good attitude

whenever you wish—let go of your problems and frustrations and go within yourself to relive the feelings and emotions that accompany a positive attitude.

9. When I was seventeen, I worked for a man who was constantly positive, no matter what problems he experienced from time to time. Every morning he stood in front of a mirror, and pumped his fists in the air while saying, "Boy, I'm enthusiastic!" He repeated these words three times, increasing his enthusiasm and volume with each repetition. My coworkers and I laughed when he told us this. However, I was curious, and decided to try it for myself. I was amazed to find this little ritual kept me positive and enthusiastic all day long. Some of the other staff members tried it too and found it worked for them as well. I'm sure it will do the same for you.

If you've had a negative attitude for any length of time, don't expect to become an optimist overnight. It takes time and practice to change any pattern of behavior. Pay attention to your thoughts and congratulate yourself each time you find yourself thinking positively. Over time, you'll find you're thinking more positive thoughts than negative ones and will have a more optimistic and less critical view of the world. Once you've reached this point, you can start actively seeking potentially lucky opportunities.

2

◆

RELATIONSHIPS

Once a month, I have dinner with a group of friends. We are an eclectic group that includes a retired airline pilot, a shaman, a financial adviser, a professional speaker, a butcher, a shop manager, a stress-management adviser, and a retired multimillionaire. The oldest member of the group is in his late eighties and the youngest is twenty-one. Like the other members, I look forward to our dinners and have learned a great deal from all of them. Most of them work in fields that I know nothing about, and it's been fascinating to hear about their hopes, dreams, and experiences. While I've also benefited financially (some of them have used my services), the greatest benefit is the close friendships that I've made. As well as our monthly meetings, I catch up with some of the members every week or two. The one thing every member has in common is that at one time or another, we all had a chance conversation in a coffee shop with Jim, the founder of the group. Jim loves talking with people and seizes every opportunity he can to meet others. He's not bothered if the other person doesn't want to chat, but if they do, Jim enjoys the conversation. As a result, he knows more people than anyone else I know. He owns a successful business, and people describe him as lucky. It looks that way to outsiders, but over the years, he's created relationships with a wide variety of people that he can contact at any time. Once he's made a friend, he works to keep the relationship alive.

The more people you meet, the more ideas you'll be exposed to, the more opportunities you'll have, and the luckier you'll become.

Dr. Philippe Gabilliet, professor in Leadership and Personal Development at the Faculty of ESCP in Paris gave a TEDxESCP talk in 2012 called "Is Success Also a Matter of Luck?" In his talk he said: "Luck hates loneliness. It's impossible to be lucky on your own" (www.youtube.com/watch?v=pMWvlYXiWcc). I'm sure people can create or discover lucky ideas on their own, but there's no way they can receive any benefit from these ideas without dealing with others.

We all lead busy lives, and it's easy to unintentionally lose contact with friends you haven't seen for a while. Make an effort to see or phone friends whenever you can. A good way to meet new people is to join clubs and other groups and make friends there. You already have at least one thing in common with the members, which provides a good start to establishing friendships. Another good way to meet people is by volunteering to help less fortunate people in your community. Whenever possible, help other people achieve their goals. Don't do this with any expectation of a reward. Your good deeds will be noticed and will attract other people to you. Start conversations with people you meet by chance. Most will be over in a minute or two, but some will develop into conversations that could lead to friendships and lucky opportunities.

All these methods work much better than networking, a word that often has negative connotations because it makes people feel as though they're being used. The important thing is to look for friends rather than people you can use for your own purposes, which is why I prefer a personal connection rather than social media.

Choose your friends wisely; make friendships with positive, kind, compassionate, and supportive people. These people will encourage you in your efforts and will let you know when you're not doing the best you can.

Be authentic and real. You can't make good friends if you hide behind a façade in the hopes that other people will accept you into their circle. There's no need to act differently to make people like you. Good friends will accept you as you are, and you can agree to disagree on certain topics and still be friends.

You can't entirely avoid negative people. You may work with, or be related to, people who are permanently pessimistic and gloomy. These people enjoy dragging you down to their level. Don't let them succeed. Be kind and listen to them without necessarily agreeing with what they say. Refuse to get angry or annoyed no matter what they say. Usually, when they find they're not getting the response they want, they'll find someone else to emotionally drain. That said, don't ignore them, either. Smile, maybe offer them a cookie or some other small treat, and praise them on their achievements. In other words, be pleasant and kind but avoid buying into their toxic attitudes.

You can have as many friends as you want by becoming interested in other people. Most people want to talk about themselves. If you encourage them to do so and listen to what they tell you, you'll gain plenty of friends and your opportunities for luck will expand enormously.

3

✦

GRATITUDE

Gratitude is the quality of feeling appreciative and thankful for what one has. It comes from the Latin *gratus*, which means "thankful" or "grateful." The Roman statesman and orator Cicero (106–43 BCE), said "Gratitude is not only the greatest of all virtues, but the parent of all the others."

Earl Nightingale (1921–1989), the American speaker and writer, believed that "the luckiest people on earth" were "those who have developed an almost constant sense of gratitude" (Nightingale 329). He was referring to people who take nothing for granted, and are grateful for the blessings and opportunities they have in life. Obviously, like everyone else, they have problems and difficulties in their lives, but they focus on the positive rather than the negative.

There is scientific evidence that shows how positive feelings of gratitude can be. Psychologists Robert Emmons and Michael McCullough asked three groups of people to write a single sentence in a journal every week for ten weeks. The first group recorded five things they were grateful for. The second group wrote five things they were unhappy about, and the third group wrote down five neutral events that had happened during the week. The people who wrote down things they were grateful for were more optimistic and positive than the people in the other two groups. They also appeared to be healthier, as they'd exercised more than the others. They were also estimated to be 25 percent happier than the members of the other two groups. (Emmons and McCullough, 2003). Dr. Robert Emmons is the world's leading researcher of gratitude and the benefits it produces. He is professor of Psychology at the University of California Davis, and has written three popular books on gratitude. (See Bibliography and Suggested Reading.)

Other benefits of gratitude include increased self-esteem, feelings of happiness and optimism; improved emotional and physical health; better relationships; more friendships; strengthened heart and immune system; increased ability to forgive; reduction in stress, anxiety, and depression; better sleep; greater motivation; and increased spirituality. In other words, gratitude increases well-being.

Gratitude is usually associated with expressing appreciation for something someone has done for you. However, it's much more than that. You can express your gratitude for a beautiful day, for health, for enough to eat, and for the sheer joy of being alive. You can be grateful for the simplest things, such as the sound of children playing or the sight of a beautiful flower. When you express gratitude, you send out feelings of abundance to the universe. The universe responds by sending back more abundance. I used to be puzzled by this line in the Bible: "For whosoever hath, to him shall be given, and he shall have more abundance, but whosoever hath not, from him shall be taken away even that he hath" (Matthew 13:12). However, its meaning becomes clear when you consider that by sending out feelings of gratitude, you become a magnet that attracts more to you. As a result of this, your luck increases. This is the law of attraction.

Saying thank you with sincerity is the most obvious way to express gratitude. You can also express gratitude with your body language and small—or large—acts of kindness. If you constantly remind yourself of the big things you're grateful for, you'll find that small problems and petty annoyances will cease to have any effect on you.

Former president of the American Psychological Association Dr. Martin Seligman created a gratitude exercise called the three blessings: at the end of every day, think about the three things that occurred during the day which you're most happy about. He found that this simple technique helped reduce feelings of anxiety and depression and at the same time increase feelings of joy and happiness. (http://www.healthassociatesllc.com/files/1352751786 .pdf) I usually think about what I'm grateful for while lying in bed at night, and fall asleep quickly and happily.

One of the best ways to increase your gratitude for the blessings in your life is to keep a gratitude journal. Every day, write three to five things in it for which you are grateful. Doing this will immediately make you feel good, no matter what sort of day you've had. The gift of life, the love of family and friends, and good health are examples of general things to be grateful for. And when you start looking, you'll also find numerous small things you're grateful for in your everyday life, such as someone holding a door open for you or a friend calling to see how you are. When I worked as sales manager for a printing company, my secretary would bring me a cup of coffee at about 10 a.m. every morning. I always thanked her, but at the time I'm sure I took it for granted even though I was grateful. Today I would definitely express my appreciation and write it down in my journal. It's important to recall as many of the small acts as possible; they're quickly forgotten otherwise. Once you start looking for things to write in your journal, you'll start feeling thankful more and more until it becomes part of your way of life.

You can take this a step further by writing letters of gratitude to people who have helped and supported you. One amazing example is John Kralik, author of *365 Thank Yous: The Year a Simple Act of Daily Gratitude Changed My Life*. In December 2007, John was a fifth-three-year-old, overweight, divorced, broke attorney. On New Year's Day, while hiking in the hills of Los Angeles, he decided to stop thinking about his problems and focus on what he was grateful for. He decided to write 365 thank you notes. He managed to do this, writing each note by hand, and almost immediately every area of his life started turning around. He writes: "Gratitude presses outwards and that creates good feelings in the universe. A lot of that comes back to you eventually."

Expressing gratitude has the power to change your life and will provide you with opportunities that you'd never have found otherwise.

4

◆

Curiosity

Curiosity is a state of mind that allows you to be extremely interested in something. In his book, *Chase, Chance, and Creativity*, James H. Austin wrote: "If we allow that necessity is the mother of invention, then curiosity is surely the father" (Austin, 108).

All parents and teachers are familiar with the seemingly endless questions their children ask. This is natural, as children are curious and want to learn. It's largely due to curiosity that we enjoy the quality of life we have today. If people hadn't been curious and asked questions, most of the things we take for granted might not have been invented. Many animals are curious, too. If you've ever had a dog or cat as a pet, you'll know how they examine and sniff anything they come across that is new or different. However, their curiosity extends only to the physical objects they happen to see or smell. Human beings are the only species who are curious about both intangible and tangible things.

People who consider themselves lucky deliberately seek out opportunities to meet new people, try new things, to travel, and to learn. They're curious about everything, and are willing to move well outside their comfort zones. My brother-in-law has become extremely successful because he's curious and asks questions about everything. He's not afraid to ask the questions that other people don't because they feel it will make them look stupid. He's become a wealthy man by asking the questions and thinking about the answers.

Curious people are willing to leave their comfort zones and try something new, different, or challenging. For instance, they might take up a new hobby, go back to school, take up a new sport, or talk to people who are doing something they'd like to try. Many years ago, I tracked down a man who made handmade paper and learned how to do it myself. Apart from making a few reams of paper, I've done nothing with this skill—but it satisfied my curiosity.

Albert Einstein (1879–1955) told his biographer Carl Seelig: "I have no special talents. I am only passionately curious. (Einstein Archives 39-013, www.alberteinstein .info/). Most geniuses are curious. In fact, it would be hard to name one who isn't, as they spend their lives questioning the status quo, investigating new and different possibilities, and enjoying the stimulation and excitement that each new idea brings. They take nothing for granted, enjoying the mental stimulation of seeking answers to their questions, and discovering new ways of doing things.

Curious people don't get bored—there's a limitless number of topics they can explore and learn about. They read books, attend seminars, ask questions, and research to learn and find answers to their questions. This broadens their knowledge and makes them interesting companions. When they meet people, they immediately want to know all about them. As most people like talking about themselves, they welcome this attention, and friendships can develop as a result. As Dale Carnegie wrote: "You can make more friends in two months by becoming interested in other people than you can in two years by trying to get other people interested in you" (Carnegie, 56).

Curiosity causes changes in the chemistry of the brain which makes it easier to learn and retain the information. A study conducted at the University of California Davis in 2014 showed nineteen volunteers one hundred questions. The volunteers were asked to rate the questions by how curious they were to learn the answers. The questions included "What Beatles single lasted longest on the charts, at nineteen weeks?" and "Who was the president of the United States when Uncle Sam first got a beard?" They were then shown the answers while their brain activity was monitored. When the volunteers were curious about the answer, the pleasure centers of their brains lit up and there was also an increased activity in the hippocampus, which is involved in the formation of memories. While this was going on, the volunteers also experienced a natural high caused by the release of dopamine. Dopamine is also related to memory retention. After this, the volunteers were shown the questions again, and the volunteers who were curious about the largest number of questions remembered the greatest number of answers (Gruber, Gelman, and Ranganath, October 22, 2014, www.cell.com/neuron/fulltext/S0896-6273(14)00804-6).

Here are five ways to develop your sense of curiosity.

1. Be enthusiastic and ask plenty of questions. Everyone responds to enthusiasm. A year ago, a club that my wife belongs to put on a dinner for their partners. After dinner, I started talking with a man who had a model railway in his backyard. I was intrigued and asked him numerous questions about his hobby. On the way home, my wife commented that the man I'd been speaking to was extremely reticent and hardly ever spoke at the committee meetings. After I'd shown my interest and asked a few questions, the man hardly stopped talking; I assume it was because it was rare for him to find anyone interested in his field of expertise. I learned a great deal and thoroughly enjoyed the conversation.

2. Whenever you're in a library or bookstore, browse through sections that are unrelated to what you're looking for. You'll always find at least one book—and probably several—that will expose you to new ideas that you can use. If you do this regularly, you'll be amazed at how rapidly your general knowledge will increase, and you may find some lucky ideas along the way.

3. Talk to people wherever you happen to be. Everyone has a story to tell, and will usually be pleased to share it with someone who appears interested. A good way to start is to ask people, "What's the most interesting thing you've done in the last few days?"

4. Be willing to ask "dumb" questions. Most people are afraid to do this, preferring to remain silent. In actuality, these types of questions are often the best way to learn.

5. Be open-minded. You won't learn anything new about a subject if you're biased or antagonistic. Some years ago, I visited a naturopath, and in the course of the appointment, mentioned that I was a hypnotherapist. She immediately said there was no such thing as hypnosis, and I should find another career. She missed out on an opportunity to learn about something she obviously knew nothing about. In my twenties, I met a beekeeper, and as a

result of that, soon had three hives of my own. That wouldn't have happened if I'd assumed it was a job for professionals, and amateurs were excluded.

Curiosity is a useful quality to possess for many reasons. Naturally, it is mentally stimulating and improves the quality of the brain. However, it also increases empathy, strengthens relationships, increases happiness, eliminates boredom, enhances creativity, decreases anxiety, and provides countless opportunities for good luck.

5

Affirmations

Affirmations are strong statements that are repeated frequently to instill positive thoughts into our minds. They're almost always phrased in the present tense, as if you already have the quality you desire. They're also said strongly and enthusiastically to add power to the words.

One of the most famous affirmations was created more than one hundred years ago by Émile Coué (1857–1926), the French psychologist who popularized autosuggestion. It is: "Every day, in every way, I'm getting better and better." That is a general affirmation. "I'm worthy of the very best life has to offer," "I attract good things to me," and "I'm alive, I'm well, and I feel great" are other examples of general affirmations.

Many affirmations are intended to work on a particular aspect of the person's life. Someone who wants to improve financially might say: "I attract wealth and abundance," "I deserve to be wealthy," "I always have enough money," or "I'm a magnet for money." An athlete might affirm: "I'm a super fit footballer (or whatever activity it happens to be) and I perform well under pressure," "I'm a winner," or "I love to win." A salesperson could say: "I'm a good sales-person and every day I'm getting better and better," "Every rejection brings me closer to my next sale," or "I'm in tune with the needs of my customers." Someone who was study-ing for exams might affirm: "I have excellent concentration and a perfect memory." Someone who wanted more confi-dence might say: "I'm calm, relaxed, and full of confidence in every type of situation." If you want more happiness in your life, you could affirm: "I feel joy and contentment every day," "I find joy and happiness in everything life has to offer," or "I choose to be a positive, happy person."

We all have thousands of thoughts a day and have no idea how many are positive, neutral, or negative. If you're thinking more positive thoughts a day than negative ones, you'll feel happy about your life and your circumstances. Of course the opposite applies, too—you're unlikely to feel happy if you're thinking more negative thoughts than pos-itive ones. Affirmations encourage you to think positively, as you're consciously repeating the words to make them a permanent part of your life.

We're unintentionally creating affirmations all the time in everyday life. If you constantly think negative thoughts, such as "life isn't fair" or "I'm never lucky," that will become your reality. Whenever you find yourself thinking negative thoughts, deliberately start thinking of something positive. You might turn the negative thought around, or maybe think of something that makes you feel positive and happy. If you started by affirming, "I'm a lucky person," and then thought of several blessings in your life, you'd gradually discover subtle changes occurring in your life. A positive affirmation said strongly and frequently will always overpower negativity.

All the same, you need to keep alert. How many times have you said, "I can't afford it"? That's one negative affirmation I remember my mother saying frequently. If you ever say or think anything like that, you should immediately tell yourself, "I'd like to have that, and I'm going to start saving for it right away."

You'll find an almost unlimited selection of affirmations online, and they all work well. I enjoy writing my own, and recommend you try this, especially if you can't find exactly what you're looking for. To do this, think about areas of your life that you'd like to change. Turn any negatives into positives, and jot down any ideas that come to you. Make sure the affirmation is believable and realistic. If you're currently working for minimum pay, for instance, it would not be a good idea to affirm that you're earning hundreds of thousands of dollars a year unless you had a clear idea on how you were going to do it. A more modest goal would prove helpful, and the figure involved could change from time to time as you reached your goals.

Write your affirmations on cards that you can carry around with you. Read them whenever you have a spare moment. Whenever possible, I like to say my affirmations out loud using as much feeling as I can. I emphasize a different word every time I say the affirmation; I whisper them, sing them in a funny voice, or even shout them at the top of my lungs, if the situation allows it. Obviously, if I was riding on a bus, sitting in a busy office, or waiting for a movie to start, I'd repeat them silently.

Some people like to write down their affirmations every day and think about each word as they write it. They pay attention to how they feel as they write the words and usually notice their state of mind gradually improving as their subconscious accepts the thought contained in the affirmation.

I mentioned that affirmations are almost always stated in the present tense, as if you already have the quality you desire. There are a few exceptions to this. If you're using affirmations to help lose weight, for instance, you might find it hard to affirm: "I am slim and sylph-like." However, you could affirm: "I'm becoming lighter day by day and I'll achieve my goal by September 30." The same thing applies to any other affirmation that sounds impossible to you when you consider your current circumstances.

Affirmations work because they program the brain into believing that they're true. The mind doesn't know the difference between reality and your affirmation. Consequently, repeating your affirmations regularly every day encourages your mind to act on these positive thoughts and make them a reality. Affirmations will help you attract good luck as a result of these positive changes. You can reinforce this by regularly affirming: "I'm a lucky person," "I create my own good luck," and "I'm constantly surrounded by good luck."

It's a simple process to create your own affirmations.

1. Write down a negative belief you have about yourself. If you feel you're lacking in confidence, you might write: "I lack confidence."

2. On a separate sheet of paper rewrite these words as if you already possess the quality you lack. In our example, you might write: "I am confident," or maybe, "I have all the confidence I need." If you feel you lack confidence in a certain area of your life, you can add that to your affirmation.

3. Destroy the negative belief. You can do this any way you like. You might scribble over it to make it totally illegible. You could shred it, burn it, or throw it away. Enjoy the process of getting rid of it, as it has no relevance in your life anymore.

4. Read the affirmation you created out loud. If it feels totally unrealistic or impossible, you'll experience tension in your body. If this occurs, ask yourself why. You might have to modify the affirmation to turn it into a believable goal.

5. Once you're happy with your affirmation, repeat it as often as you can, silently and out loud, during the day.

Repeat your affirmations, silently or out loud, whenever you have a spare moment. You might say them silently while waiting in line somewhere, or out loud while sitting in your car waiting for the traffic light to change. Affirmations have helped many people increase their luck and achieve their goals. They can do the same for you.

6

◆

Contentment

Contentment is an emotional state of satisfaction and peace of mind. It means you accept yourself for the person you are, and you're satisfied with what you have. You no longer compare yourself to others and feel grateful for all the gifts that life has to offer. You accept others as they are, and this increases your opportunities for love and friendship. You express gratitude for what you have, and are not concerned with what you don't have. Your life is simpler, richer, and happier as a result.

Contentment leads to happiness, but the two words are not synonymous. Happiness is difficult to define. Some people feel they'd be happy if they had plenty of money. Others consider love, good health, travel, or achieving a specific goal to be examples of happiness. All of these things can contribute to happiness, but none of them are essential qualities. Stimulating moments, such as a good meal, passionate sex, a pay rise, or trying a new experience, provide temporary pleasure and joy but do not provide lasting happiness.

Contentment is more long-lasting than happiness. Happiness occurs when a desire is met, while contentment is a feeling of gratitude and peace of mind. Consequently, happiness tends to come in moments, while contentment is a state of mind that can be sustained indefinitely.

Contented people do receive more luck in life. This is because people with positive attitudes expect opportunities to come their way and they're ready to take advantage of them when they do. In addition, contented people are more likely to enjoy successful relationships, have greater job satisfaction, earn more money, enjoy greater physical and mental health, and live longer than people who lack these benefits. They're also more likely to help others, as they receive pleasure and satisfaction from their altruism. They have more friends, bounce back from setbacks quickly, and smile and laugh much more than people who lack contentment in their lives. When you look at the benefits that contented people receive, it's no wonder they're considered lucky.

Here are seven ways to achieve contentment.

1. Practice gratitude (see chapter 3). People who practice gratitude have learned to focus on what's good in their lives, rather than dwell on what they lack.

2. Don't compare yourself with others. There will always be people who can do something better than you or who appear to be wealthier or happier than you. However, no one can be a better you than you.

3. Help others. When you do, you'll start realizing how much wisdom you have that you can share with others.

4. Simplify your life. You'll gain a strong sense of freedom when you eliminate what you don't need. This includes people who cause you nothing but aggravation, as well as possessions you no longer need.

5. Be kind to yourself and others. You can't achieve contentment when you're running yourself down. Everyone makes mistakes. Take care with your thoughts and be compassionate and gentle with yourself. Positive affirmations (chapter 5) can help with this. Being kind to others makes you feel better about yourself, too.

6. Make room in your life for exercise. All forms of exercise release endorphins and make you feel good about yourself. You'll also look and feel good about yourself.

7. Spend time with positive people. Make sure to spend time every day with people who are enthusiastic, positive, and supportive. Their optimistic outlook will

rub off on you, and make you feel good, no matter what sort of day you're having.

Be content with what you have, and live in the moment. At the same time, continue learning, growing, and developing. You can experience contentment and remain alert for lucky opportunities.

7

◆

Persistence

Everyone experiences times when things don't go according to plan or don't work out as well as expected. Many people give up in such circumstances and instead search for something that is less demanding and easier to attain. Unfortunately, people who quit easily seldom achieve much in life. The people who persist despite failures, adversities, and other problems are the ones who usually succeed in the end.

Many successful people can attribute their success to persistence. Academics study long and hard for many years to achieve success. Many people have to work hard to achieve academic qualifications before starting their careers. People who achieved fame in any sport spent countless hours developing their skills. Business people usually struggle before achieving success. It took James Dyson fifteen years to perfect the vacuum cleaner that made him famous. Along the way, he failed 5,127 times. However, he persisted and is now worth more than five billion dollars. More than a thousand people rejected Colonel Sanders's fried chicken recipe before he finally achieved success at the age of fifty-six. Thomas Edison had to perform more than ten thousand experiments before creating the light bulb. Henry Ford failed in business five times before starting one of the world's most successful automotive companies. Abraham Lincoln is another remarkable example of someone who persisted despite numerous setbacks.

Persistent people believe in themselves. They know what they want, make a plan to achieve it, and then work steadily until they've achieved their goal. Naturally, they take time out for rest and relaxation, and socialize with like-minded people, but once they've done that, they return to their goal. They think long-term and refuse to give up, no matter what delays and setbacks they experience along the way. They might reevaluate their plans, and change direction if necessary, but they won't give up. They persist until they've achieved their goal.

Persistent people are often considered lucky by others. People who quit after one or two setbacks consider their failure to be "bad luck" and the persistent person's success to be nothing but "good luck."

Dr. Martin Luther King Jr. (1929–1968) had to be persistent in his fight for civil rights. When he spoke at a college rally in 1960, he said: "If you can't fly, then run; if you can't run, then walk, if you can't walk; then crawl, but whatever you do, you have to keep moving forward" (https://kinginstitute.stanford.edu/king-papers/documents /keep-moving-mountain-address-spelman-college-10 -april-1960.)

However, there are also times when it's better to quit than persist against impossible odds. A friend of mine owned a small sporting magazine that did well for many years. However, the introduction of the internet made it possible for his readers to obtain the information they wanted without subscribing to his magazine. He tried an online version of his magazine, which never took off. He persisted until his business failed. It would have been better for him and his family if he'd given it his best shot, decided it wasn't enough, and closed his magazine before he was forced to. He bounced back after that setback, though, and today he's using his skills to help people produce and self-publish their books.

There's a technique to determine when you should persist, and when you should change your focus.

1. Set aside twenty to thirty minutes when you won't be disturbed. Place paper and pen, or some form of recording device, on a table next to a comfortable chair. Sit down in the chair, close your eyes, and relax. You might find it helpful to focus on your breathing and silently say, "calm and relaxed" each time you exhale.

2. After a couple of minutes, mentally scan your body to make sure you are completely relaxed. Focus on any areas of tension until you feel them let go and relax.

3. When you feel completely relaxed, think about your present situation and the goal you're trying to achieve. Ask yourself if it's worth persisting with this goal. Mentally scan your body again to see if you're still fully relaxed. If not, focus on any areas of tension until they let go, before moving on to the next step.

4. In your mind's eye, visualize yourself three months in the future, and "see" what the situation will be like. Scan your body again, and if it's relaxed, move forward six months, and then twelve.

5. Return to the present moment, and visualize yourself sitting in your comfortable chair with your eyes closed. Ask yourself: "Should I continue on the path I'm on now, or is it time to let go of this goal and focus on something else?" Ask further questions, if any.

6. Ask yourself: "Is there anything else I need to know about where to go from here?"

7. Allow yourself to enjoy a minute or two of quiet relaxation, and then mentally count from one to five and open your eyes.

8. As soon as you can after opening your eyes, write down everything that came into your mind during the exercise.

You may have to repeat this exercise a number of times to get all the answers you need. If your subconscious mind tells you to continue on the path you're on, you'll have to use all the persistence you can muster to push forward until you achieve success. Conversely, if the advice is to change direction, you can perform this exercise again as many times as necessary while asking questions about what you should do instead. While some people are naturally persistent, it is a skill that anyone can develop.

8

✦

Passion

American singer-songwriter Jon Bon Jovi said, "Nothing is as important as passion. No matter what you want to do with your life, be passionate" (Stulberg and Magness, 13). Passion provides energy, purpose, enthusiasm, excitement, and zest for life. It enables you to achieve whatever it is you want in life, and ensures you receive the maximum amount of enjoyment while you are alive. Passionate people have a purpose in life, and this is obvious in everything they do.

Have you ever been told to follow your passion or pursue something that you love or are extremely enthusiastic about? A 2013 Gallup poll revealed that 85 percent of people worldwide dislike or even hate their jobs and only 13 percent were passionate about their work (https://news.gallup.com /poll/165269/worldwide-employees-engaged-work.aspx). It's sad that so few people make a career out of their passions. These people drag themselves to work on Monday morning.

Passionate people can't wait to get back to work. Passionate people love what they do; it improves every aspect of their lives and increases their chances of luck.

Here's an example. Passionate people are much more likely to be promoted than colleagues who are doing the minimum amount of work they can get away with to keep their jobs. The latter people are likely to view the former's promotion as good luck and overlook their enthusiasm, attitude, and work ethic. Passionate people always do more than what's expected of them.

Unfortunately, many people haven't found anything that they're passionate about. Some people are fortunate and know what they want to do with their lives at an early age, but most people don't. The answer is to find something that you enjoy and learn as much as possible about it. Hopefully, you'll find your interest will grow and develop, and will ultimately turn into a passion. One of my high school teachers told us that he became a teacher because he was interested in education and became more and more passionate about it as he studied and learned more. He told us: "Choose something you enjoy and the passion will come."

Some people find their passion by chance, while others have to search to find it. Here are some ways to find your passion.

1. You're awake for about sixteen hours a day. What do you do with those hours? It's possible that you already have a passion but haven't recognized it yet.

2. Check your credit card statements. They'll tell you what you're interested in. Evaluate each purchase to see if it could be or eventually become a passion.

3. Think about the various hobbies and interests you've been interested in from early childhood up to the present. Do you feel a spark of excitement when you recall a hobby or interest from the past? Could you turn this into a career, or avocation?

4. Do you read nonfiction books, or maybe enjoy watching documentaries on TV? The subjects you read or watch may give you clues about your passion. Look at the books on your shelves, and, while you're doing that, examine your magazines and DVDs for clues.

5. Spend an hour or two in a library or large bookstore. Be open-minded and spend time in sections that you've never browsed in before. Pick up any books that interest you.

6. Browse the internet. Start by searching for a topic that interests you, and see where the various links take you. Do a search for hobbies and investigate any that seem interesting.

7. Spend time with good friends and ask them what they think you'd be good at. Tell them you're trying to find your passion and ask for ideas. You may be

surprised at some of the suggestions you receive. While doing this, ask them to tell you what you most like to talk about.

8. Create passion for yourself. If you put your heart and soul into everything you do, you'll quickly have so many ideas you won't know what to do with them all.

9. Ask yourself questions. What truly matters to you? What excites you? What would you do if you were independently wealthy and could do anything you wanted? Who, or what, inspires you?

On October 26, 1967, six months before he was assassinated, Dr. Martin Luther King Jr. gave a talk at Barratt Junior High School in Philadelphia. Although he didn't mention the word, he gave a striking example of the passion he wanted the students to develop. He said: "If it falls your lot to be a street sweeper, sweep streets like Michelangelo painted pictures, sweep streets like Beethoven composed music, sweep streets like Leontyne Price sings before the Metropolitan Opera. Sweep streets like Shakespeare wrote poetry. Sweep streets so well that all the hosts of heaven and earth will have to pause and say: 'Here lived a great street sweeper who swept his job well.'"(King, 1992)

Passion is infectious, and people are attracted to passionate people because they're full of energy, enthusiasm, and zest for life. Naturally, they attract other people who share their passion, and they also meet people with different passions. These seemingly chance encounters can provide fruitful, lucky opportunities.

Passion is a state of mind. You can develop passion by becoming more interested in what you're doing. See if you can find ways to do your work better and more efficiently. You'll come up with creative ideas that you can introduce to help the organization you work for. By doing this, you'll become more motivated and enthusiastic about your work. You'll develop a more positive personality. You'll also enjoy your work more and will seek opportunities to demonstrate your particular skills. You'll find yourself working harder and receiving more enjoyment from your work. If you do all of this, you'll be noticed, and it won't be long before you're promoted or given more responsibility as well as a pay rise. When you reach this stage, your work colleagues will talk about how lucky you are.

9

◆

Imagination

Imagination is one of the greatest forces in the world. If humans didn't possess this quality, the world as we know it could not exist. Everything that has been invented or created began in someone's imagination. When you imagine something, you're using your mind to create a mental picture of something that has not been perceived through the usual five senses. Your imagination is limitless, and you can use it to travel anywhere and to do anything. One of Albert Einstein's most famous quotes is: "Imagination is more important than knowledge. For knowledge is limited, whereas imagination embraces the entire world, stimulating progress, giving birth to evolution" (Einstein, 97).

We start exercising our imaginations in early childhood, listening to stories and playing games. Unfortunately, we often lose the incredible joy that our imaginations can provide as we get older. We can learn a great deal from watching children play, because as adults, we tend to regard life as a serious business and rely more on facts and figures than the richness we already have in our imaginations.

There are various types of imagination. One form occurs when you take two or more existing ideas and combine them in a new, original way to create something different. You can use your imagination and your logical mind to consciously work out a solution to a problem. Henry Ford did this when he developed an affordable motorcar. You can use your imagination to daydream and fantasize something new and original. This usually starts from an inspiration that is played with and developed in the mind. Fiction writers do this when they create their stories. Most people can use their imaginations to sense what other people are feeling or experiencing. Not surprisingly, this is called empathic imagination. Some people are good at spotting opportunities and visualizing how they could develop or capitalize on it. I have a friend who buys badly managed businesses, builds them up, and sells them two or three years later for a large profit. He has an unerring knack for seeing potential that most people overlook.

Our imaginations are possibly at their best when we're dreaming. You might like to keep a pen and paper, or some form of recording device, beside your bed to enable you to record your dreams before they permanently disappear. The plot of *The Strange Case of Dr. Jekyll and Mr. Hyde* came to Robert Louis Stevenson in a feverish dream. He had many of these bouts as he suffered from consumption (tuberculosis). He was angry when his wife woke him and he lost much of the story. Fortunately, he remembered enough to develop it into his famous novel.

Niels Bohr (1885–1962), the Danish physicist, discovered the structure of the atom in a dream in which he saw the nucleus of the atom surrounded by electrons spinning around it. He researched this idea and found it was true. In 1922, he received the Nobel Peace Prize for his discovery.

Your imagination can increase your luck if you harness and use it. Daydreaming is a pleasant way to relax, but if you don't do anything with the ideas that come into your mind, you're nothing but a dreamer. To create luck, you need to harness your ideas and act on them.

Developing your natural curiosity is a good way to increase your luck. Children are good at asking questions, but adults frequently don't do this as they don't want to be considered ignorant or stupid. However, asking questions is a good way to learn, and the answers you receive will stimulate your imagination and creativity.

Spending time talking or brainstorming with creative friends and acquaintances is a good way to learn, develop your own creativity, and find lucky opportunities.

Learning more about subjects that interest you will help you advance in your career or avocation. Doing this will also expose you to new ideas and concepts that you can develop further using your creativity and imagination.

Taking up a new hobby or investigating a subject that has always interested you is a good way to open your mind to new ideas that might prove useful. It can be highly rewarding to expose yourself to new ideas and concepts. It expands your imagination and encourages you to explore different areas of interest. A friend of mine took up the flute in his late forties. He did this because he wanted something to help him relax after working all day at a stressful job. It worked so well that he started a small orchestra that performs regularly to raise money for different charities. He is now retired from the workforce but still actively involved with his orchestra. He also teaches the flute part-time, and regularly plays the flute in theatrical productions. He credits the instrument with saving his life. He's also made many new friends and has started composing. Taking up a new interest transformed his life.

Read as much as you can. This stimulates your imagination and encourages creativity. If you do this, you'll soon have more ideas than you know what to do with. Evaluate these carefully and learn more about ideas that especially interest you. You need to act on only one good idea for everyone to call you lucky.

Spend time on your own every day to sit down comfortably, close your eyes, and relax. Relaxation helps diffuse all the built-up tension and anxiety that our bodies carry. It's hard to be imaginative or creative when your body is carrying all this unnecessary baggage. While in this calm, peaceful, quiet, relaxed state, think about your goals and what you want to achieve in this lifetime. Allow your mind to flow freely and entertain any ideas that occur to you. This technique is also a useful way to find answers to questions and discover solutions to problems.

Going outside your comfort zone is an excellent way to develop your imagination. If you seldom talk to strangers, for instance, try talking to someone at the table next to you next time you go out for coffee (but not if the person appears to be working, of course). You could exchange a few words with people you encounter during the day, maybe while waiting in line, sitting on a bus, or when you're out walking. Some conversations will finish after exchanging a few pleasantries, but every now and again you'll enjoy a good conversation that might lead to friendship. Nevertheless, these conversations will always give you good ideas.

A lady I know had a fear of heights. For her fortieth birthday, she booked a parachute jump without telling any of her family or friends. She was terrified, but skydiving cured her of her fear. She's done several more jumps since and wrote an article on how she overcame her fear that was published in a community newspaper. She now writes a monthly column for them. If she hadn't stepped outside her comfort zone, this would never have happened.

You have an excellent imagination. If you keep your imagination stimulated, sooner or later you'll have a brilliant idea, and everyone will start talking about how lucky you are.

10

◆

Expanding
Your Mind

Education is the process of imparting or acquiring knowledge and understanding. It expands the mind. It also involves making mistakes and learning from them. Ideally, education should be a lifelong pursuit rather than something that mainly happens in schools and other places of learning. Thanks to libraries and the internet, information is freely available to almost everyone nowadays. You can become an expert in any subject you wish by using the local library or going online. In a speech given on July 16, 2003, former South African President Nelson Mandela (1918–2013) said: "Education is the most powerful weapon which you can use to change the world." (http://db.nelsonmandela .org/speeches/pub_view.asp?pg=item&ItemID=NMS909)

"If a man empties his purse into his head, no man can take it away from him. An investment in knowledge pays the best interest." This quote is generally credited to Benjamin Franklin (1706–1790). However, the first printed record of it appeared almost fifty years after his death (*The Daily Evening Transcript*, Boston, November 29, 1848. Page 1, col. 5.). Whether or not it was coined by Benjamin Franklin, it encompasses a wealth of information in just a few words. It says that anything that has been learned cannot be taken away. Therefore, any form of education is a good investment. The word "knowledge" in the quote refers to more than academic study. Any form of learning is beneficial, as it stimulates the brain, exposes you to new ideas and concepts, adds to your skill set, and increases your knowledge of the world. Different forms of learning include apprenticeships, trade schools, on the job learning, experience, finding a mentor, and self-study such as reading books or watching online courses. Learning encompasses much more than training for a career. As you progress through life you may choose to learn about such subjects as sports, hobbies, relationships, home maintenance, child-rearing, and computer programming. None of these may pay off financially, but they'll enrich you in many other ways.

Learning is much more enjoyable when you're motivated and interested in the subject. You'll find you'll learn what you want to know quickly and easily. You'll ask yourself questions about what you read or hear and will voluntarily search out the answers. It's not as easy if the topic is something you're not especially interested in but need to learn for a specific reason. In this instance, you'll need to find a strong reason to persist and learn whatever it is you need to know. One good way to do this is to search for ways to relate the new material to subjects that interest you. Many years ago, I did a series of talks on mythology and found it hard to memorize what I needed to know about Norse mythology. I've always been interested in divination, and learning Norse mythology became considerably easier when I discovered I could relate the different myths to the twenty-four early Futhark runes.

If you're studying for an exam or some other purpose, set aside specific times for study. If you decide to study from seven p.m. to nine p.m. every night, stick to that schedule until it becomes a habit. Find a quiet place to work, and make sure you won't be interrupted for the length of time you've set. Study for thirty to forty minutes, and then have a five- or ten-minute break before starting to study again. Memory expert Dr. Ken Kern recommends washing your face during this break, as it "will increase your energy and re-charge your brain, priming it for even more learning" (Kern, 63). He also suggests standing up from time to time while you're studying, as it increases your ability to learn new information. Keep on top of your thinking, and reward yourself every now and again, especially when you pass certain milestones. Constantly remind yourself how happy you'll be once you've passed the exam, gained a particular qualification, or learned a new skill.

You are your most important asset. Your education didn't finish when you left school—no matter how old you may be, continue investing in yourself. Every bit of learning you do will pay off handsomely, including by increasing your ability to attract good luck.

11

◆

Generosity

People who are generous give freely to others without thinking of any reward. They give money, objects, time, and help. These people usually demonstrate generosity of spirit, too, and are kind and gentle in their dealings with others. Generosity is most evident when natural disasters occur. During difficult times, people and nations are more than willing to offer their time, talents, resources, and money. All the major religions stress the importance of helping others. The Bible says: "And though I have the gift of prophecy, and understand all mysteries, and all knowledge; and though I have all faith, so that I could remove mountains, and have not charity, I am nothing" (1 Corinthians 13:2). Jesus said: "It is more blessed to give than to receive" (Acts 20:35).

Generous people have a number of traits in common. They are altruistic, which means they have an unselfish concern for the welfare and happiness of others. They give from the heart. They care for humanity as a whole. They are optimists and believe that the good they do makes the world a better place. They're willing to put time and energy into helping others. Generous people are usually humble, and give quietly to causes they believe in. They give without expecting or requiring any return. They often seek out opportunities to help others. Generous people prefer to give, rather than to receive. Generous people also practice gratitude—because they're grateful for all the blessings in their lives, they want to share with others (see chapter 3).

One final trait that generous people possess is that they're happier than people who aren't. There is a large amount of scientific research to confirm this. A 2018 experiment by researchers at Zurich University found that even promising to be generous affects the altruistic parts of the brain and makes people happier. They also found that the amount of generosity had no effect on the increase in happiness. Consequently, even small acts of generosity have a positive effect on the brain (https://www.nature.com/articles/ncomms15964).

It's not surprising that generous people are happier than others, as they receive pleasure from the act of giving. The English poet John Dryden (1631–1700) wrote: "The secret pleasure of a generous act is the great mind's bribe" (Dryden, 429).

Generous people also receive more than their share of good luck. In her book, *The Creative Habit*, Twyla Tharp, the American dancer and choreographer, wrote: "I cannot overstate how much a generous spirit contributes to good luck. Look at the luckiest people around you, the ones you envy, the ones who seem to have destiny falling habitually into their laps. If they're anything like the fortunate people I know, they're prepared, they're always working at their craft, they're alert, they involve their friends in their work, and they tend to make others feel lucky to be around them" (Tharp, 137).

Another reason generous people are lucky is that they treat others well. Because of this, people talk about them, recommend them to others, and offer them opportunities that they wouldn't offer to other people. They don't let their egos get in the way when dealing with others. They'll happily listen to other people who need to build themselves up, but refuse to do it themselves.

If you look, you'll find opportunities to be generous everywhere you go. Your family, friends, neighbors, work colleagues, local community, and town or city all need help every now and again. The poet Henry Wadsworth Longfellow (1807–1882) said: "Give what you have. To someone, it may be better than you dare to think" (Gale, 130).

You might support a local charity. You could do this by donating to them on a regular basis, or by volunteering to help. You might visit someone in hospital, or offer to do the shopping for a sick neighbor. You might spend time with someone who is hurting or lonely. You might teach English to an immigrant, or use a skill you possess to help others. I used to entertain children in hospital with magic tricks, and derived enormous pleasure from doing it. I know several people who regularly perform random acts of kindness, such as paying for someone's lunch, or paying the toll for the car behind them.

You might decide to do something big to help your community. I recently saw an interview on TV about a woman who had set up a center where lonely or unemployed people in her town could go for a coffee and a chat. She started with a handful of people, but word quickly got around, and after a few months the local council provided her with a rent-free building to accommodate the hundred or more people who came every day. Local businesses provided food and drinks, and she's now helping others set up similar centers in other towns. Start as small as you wish, and see what happens. Everything you do to help others comes back to you, and you'll find yourself rewarded in many different ways. Once you start doing this, you'll quickly see the truth in these words by John Bunyan (1628–1688): "You have not lived today until you have done something for someone who can never repay you."

Being generous means that you consider life to be full and abundant. You've discarded all thoughts of lack and scarcity. With this mindset, how can life not be plentiful and joyful? If life is so abundant, you can afford to be generous, and life will reward you for it. This is an excellent example of the law of attraction: by being generous to others, you'll receive the same in return. Your thoughts and actions will attract all the good things of life to you, and you'll have all the luck you could possibly desire.

12

◆

Responsibility

The word "responsibility" comes from the Latin *respon-sum,* which refers to someone who has to answer to someone else. Responsible people accept the consequences of everything they say and do. If something is your responsibility, it means that you are accountable, and it's your duty or job to look after whatever it happens to be. It's doing the right thing. If a task involves making important decisions, the person is said to carry a lot of responsibility. Responsible people show initiative, and motivate themselves. They like to finish what they start. Irresponsible people are the opposite and create negativity wherever they go. They cause constant problems for others, such as forgetting appointments, not caring about being late, failing to follow instructions, and doing what they feel like without caring about the consequences. Irresponsible people can sometimes be lucky, of course. However, if they won a lottery, they'd need to learn responsibility to hang on to their money. Otherwise, they'd fritter it all away. I know someone who did exactly that.

Your ability to accept responsibility tells others a great deal about you. People will notice you when you do what you say you're going to do, and they'll consider you to be an honest, reliable, and honorable person. If you make a habit of doing this, people will realize they can rely on you, and you'll be offered promotions and other opportunities as a result.

Responsibility is an essential quality for anyone who wants to progress in their career, and the higher the person rises, the more responsibilities he or she will have. Bessie Rowland James wrote: "No matter how lofty you are in your department, the responsibility for what your lowliest assistant is doing is yours" (Martin, 138). Her words are just as true today as they were more than 160 years ago.

There are a number of types of responsibility, such as personal, moral, and social responsibility. People who take personal responsibility are true to themselves. They make the most of the talents and abilities they've been blessed with. People with moral responsibility have a strong sense of right and wrong, and try to behave ethically in all of their interactions with others. An example of this would be helping people who are weak and unable to help themselves. Social responsibility is the ability to remain aware of the needs of others and the world we live in, sometimes at the expense of personal goals. Everyone makes mistakes, and responsible people are no exception. However, they accept responsibility for their mistakes, and make amends when they can. They try to find solutions to problems, rather than making excuses, or trying to blame others for any mistakes that occur.

Responsibility is a learned skill. We learn it from our parents, teachers, friends, and anyone or anything else that influenced us. If your parents were hardworking, conscientious people, chances are you will be too, as you will have learned this by watching and listening to them while you were growing up. Over the years, you gradually learned the advantages of being honest, punctual, well organized, and self-disciplined. These are all characteristics of responsible people. In addition, they don't complain or make excuses, and they freely admit it when they make mistakes. They know that trust has to be earned.

Truly responsible people are also grounded and modest. They remain steady and consistent, no matter what highs and lows occur in their lives. This can be hard to achieve, as responsible people are usually busy and often need to learn how to apportion their time wisely. To be effective in every area of their lives, it's important that they allow enough time for their families, friends, and communities, as well as for physical fitness, spiritual practices, relaxation, and recreation. They're also modest and unassuming, with no need to try to impress others. Their sense of humility enables them to bring out the best in others, and creates loyalty.

Responsible people are usually cautious, but they're willing to take calculated risks when necessary. They evaluate the situation, and consider all the possible outcomes of the different scenarios, before making a decision.

When I was in my late teens, I worked in an abattoir for a few months to save enough money to travel to the United Kingdom to further my education. The experience was eye-opening. Everyone worked at their tasks while the boss was present, but as soon as he left, almost everyone stopped working. I was rebuked because I continued doing my job. I was forced to slow down but never completely stopped working each time this occurred. On thinking about it, I came to the realization that many people cannot work without constant supervision. They are not responsible enough to do the tasks they're being paid to perform on their own. These people are invariably failures in life, as it's impossible to succeed without a sense of responsibility.

There are many benefits to being responsible. You'll make friends with other responsible people who believe in you. These friends have the potential to expose you to new opportunities. You'll also attract people who need a shoulder to lean on. This is inevitable, because responsible people can see other people's points of view, and consequently develop empathy for others. Responsible people often become leaders as others look to them for help when things go wrong. Responsible leaders think before acting, and then work as long and as hard as necessary to achieve a good solution. They also stay in control of their feelings, work well with others, and don't expect praise when the job is completed. Their satisfaction comes from successfully achieving the desired result.

With all of these qualities, it's no wonder that responsible people attract a great deal of luck as they progress through life.

13

◆

Be Inspired by Others

We all tend to copy other people's behavior, and often do this unknowingly. Two people who are in rapport will unconsciously mirror each other's posture, for instance. You may have noticed that you behave slightly differently when you're with one group of people than you do with another. I know that I reveal a different part of myself at a Kiwanis Club meeting than I do when I'm attending Salespeople with a Purpose. This is called psychological modeling. It can be done both consciously and unconsciously.

The most common reason to model yourself on someone is because they inspire you and you'd like to emulate their success. You might have dreams and goals, but if you're not making any progress in life, you may have picked up bad habits, beliefs, and behaviors that hold you back. You may not even be aware of these at a conscious level. If you're more ambitious than your friends and associates, you need to meet and associate with motivated and successful people, and be inspired by them.

You can be inspired by anyone, alive or dead. You can learn a great deal by reading books about successful people and modeling yourself on what you learn about them. When I decided to become a writer, I was inspired by the writing habits of Jack London and Erle Stanley Gardner. They wrote fiction rather than nonfiction but all the same, I found their rules of work extremely helpful when I was starting my writing career.

There are an unlimited number of people alive and dead who can motivate and inspire you to set and achieve your goals. The first step is to decide exactly what you want. It was easy in my case, as I decided to become a writer when I was ten years old. Your goals are likely to be completely different to mine. Let's assume you want to become CEO of a large corporation. Before starting, it would pay to analyze why you want to do this. There's always a price to be paid. You may need to study to gain the necessary qualifications before you start. If you're not prepared to put in the long hours, deal with the inevitable office politics, handle staff, control stress, and put up with possibly lengthy periods away from home, you'll probably decide the price is too high. If that's the case, there are other options. You might lower your sights slightly, for instance. You might choose a totally different career or decide to work for yourself.

Once you've decided on your goal, think about the people who inspire you. This might be someone you know. In this case, he or she might be kind enough to mentor you (see chapter 32). It might be someone who inspired you when you met them or heard them speak. It might be someone who happens to be your boss, or belongs to a club or organization you belong to. The person doesn't necessarily need to know that you're using them as inspiration. In fact, it's more likely that you'll model yourself on someone you read about. Read books about five or six people who've succeeded in doing what you want to do. Find out as much as you can about them (I own six biographies of Jack London), make notes as you read, and decide if you really want to model yourself on some aspect of the person. If the person is alive, you'll probably find more information in interviews, articles, and on the internet. Pay special attention to the person's answers to questions when being interviewed—they'll provide clues to the person's values and beliefs.

Even if you have the opportunity, think carefully before meeting the person, especially if there are some aspects of his or her character that you don't like. When a friend of mine started a career as an accountant, she modeled herself on the CEO of an international accounting firm. She chose him because of his rapid climb to success and because of all the favorable articles she'd read about him. However, meeting him was totally disillusioning for her—she told me he was a ruthless tyrant who yelled at his staff and played favorites. I suggested that she model the aspects of him that had appealed to her in the first place and ignore the aspects she didn't like. Instead of doing that, she researched and found a different person who, although not as successful as her first choice, had done well in her field.

You don't need to select just one person. You may prefer to choose aspects from several people rather than just one. Whatever you do, don't try to *become* the person who inspired you. Use aspects of this person's character to progress in your life but don't become a clone.

If you learn as much as you can and adapt the habits and behaviors of the right person, you'll start progressing in your career. In time, people will start modeling themselves on you. It also won't take long before people start telling you how lucky you are.

14

◆

Go the
Extra Mile

People who are prepared to go the extra mile are willing to put in extra effort to achieve excellence. This is usually done with feelings of kindness, helpfulness, and generosity. People who consistently do this achieve much more in life than people who do the least they can. It is the difference between being average and being exceptional.

You get paid for the value you provide to the organization you work for. This explains why one person makes hundreds of dollars an hour, while someone else earns minimum wage. Someone working in a factory earns a mere fraction of the income that a brain surgeon, for instance, does. Neither are being paid for the number of hours they're at work, but for the amount of value they provide while they're there. If you know more, and can do more, than another employee you'll also earn more, as you'll have additional skills to offer to a potential employer. You'll also be noticed, promoted, and considered lucky by others. The more knowledge you have (especially specialized, work-related knowledge), the more valuable you'll become. You can gain this knowledge by studying, reading, attending courses and workshops, and talking with people who already know what you need to learn. A friend of mine watches YouTube videos that relate to his career for at least an hour every evening and claims that doing this has increased his work opportunities. You increase your value to others by becoming better at everything you do.

If you're self-employed, you can increase your value to the marketplace by offering more value to whatever it is you do. The philosopher and motivational speaker Jim Rohn (1930–2009) put this very well when he said: "We get paid for bringing value to the marketplace. It takes time to bring value to the marketplace, but we get paid for the value, not the time" (Rasmusson, 32).

Going the extra mile means being honest, reliable, punctual, thoughtful, motivated, considerate, and fair, as these are all qualities that are prized in every area of life, not solely in the workforce. By embracing and making use of these qualities, as well as your skills and talents, you'll add value to everything you do.

Going the extra mile also means helping others. See if you can help someone today. It might be something small, such as a friendly smile or listening while someone gets rid of their frustration, or it could be something much larger.

You never know what will happen when you do this. You could be about to discover a lucky opportunity.

There are several things you can do to go the extra mile and demonstrate your value to your company.

1. Show initiative, and look for tasks that need to be done once you've completed your own work.

2. Strive for excellence. Always do the very best you can.

3. Try to solve problems yourself rather than passing them on to others.

4. Keep up with technology and trends. Embrace change and learn as much as you can about new developments.

5. Develop new skills and be willing to share what you've learned with others.

6. Ask for feedback. In your conversations with others, ask what you can do or learn to become better at your tasks.

7. Learn as much as you can about the industry you're in. The more you know about the business, the more useful you'll be. Share what you learn with your colleagues.

8. Always do more than your job description suggests.

9. Always exceed other people's expectations. It makes no difference if they're colleagues, customers, family members, or friends.

10. Take pride in everything you do.

You can make use of these ideas in every area of your life. Someone with a good work ethic is always valued and noticed by others. One person I spoke to about going the extra mile said it sounded exhausting. In fact, doing the best you can raises your energy, making you a valuable person to your family, friends, and coworkers.

15

Get Out of Your Comfort Zone

People are said to be in their comfort zone when they experience little stress and feel in control of the environment they're in; it's a comfortable and safe place. Stepping outside one's comfort zone exposes one to risk, stress, anxiety, and uncertainty about what will happen. Not surprisingly, most people prefer to stay safely inside their comfort zones...but the price they pay for doing so is high.

You can't achieve great goals or develop your passion without stretching yourself and taking risks. Calculated, carefully thought-out risks are essential for growth and development. As few people get everything right on their first attempt, the chances are you're likely to fail every now and again when you go outside your comfort zone, but this doesn't matter. You'll learn from the experience and can return to your comfort zone to think and evaluate before stretching yourself again.

Don't stay there too long, though. Your comfort zone is safe but drains you of motivation and energy. You'll never achieve your goals as long as you remain inside your comfort zone. A friend once told me that living in the comfort zone meant "the death of all dreams." You're unlikely to try anything new that could be stressful or demanding, which means you miss out on potentially lucky opportunities or experiences. You procrastinate, and eventually become unwilling to do anything that will take you outside your comfort zone.

In a sermon given at Ebenezer Baptist Church in Atlanta, Georgia, in 1967, Dr. Martin Luther King Jr. said:

> I say to you, this morning, that if you have never found something so dear and precious to you that you will die for it, then you aren't fit to live. You may be 38 years old, as I happen to be, and one day, some great opportunity stands before you and calls upon you to stand for some great principle, some great issue, some great cause. And you refuse to do it because you are afraid. You refuse to do it because you want to live longer. You're afraid that you will lose your job, or you are afraid that you will be criticized or that you will lose your popularity, or you're afraid

that somebody will stab or shoot or bomb your house. So you refuse to take a stand. Well, you may go on and live until you are ninety, but you are just as dead at 38 as you would be at 90. (https://www.youtube.com/watch?v =HV0Zmxa4hvw)

If you feel as though you're in a rut and need to escape your comfort zone, be brave and take a small risk. If you're single, you might decide to ask an attractive person for a date. This risk is minimal; the worst thing that could happen is that you'll be turned down. However, I know people who find it almost impossible to do this. It's particularly sad when you think of all the unattached people who'd love to be in a good relationship but are too scared to take that first step.

Speaking to a stranger could be another example of a relatively small risk. You might meet a charming person who ultimately becomes a friend. You might be rebuffed. No matter what result you get, try it again and again until you can speak to a stranger easily without anxiety or fear. Public speaking is arguably people's number one fear. If necessary, attend a public speaking course or join Toastmasters. When you feel ready, give a short speech. The mere act of doing this could change your life. A friend of mine sells insurance as a byproduct of his free talks. He almost fainted with fear when he gave his first talk. Today, he speaks several times a week and loves doing it. It's also made him a wealthy man.

Take several risks, until you've discovered that you not only survive, but become stronger every time you stretch yourself in this way. This happens no matter what the outcome of each risk is. You'll also gain confidence as you've learned that you can comfortably live with uncertainty.

Once you've taken a few risks, make a list of all the things you'd like to do. These need to be activities that involve courage and persistence. At least one of them should be something that feels totally impossible at the moment. Choose the easiest item on your list and work on achieving it first. Repeat this with another one and another one until getting out of your comfort zone provides a sense of exhilaration rather than fear.

All of these smaller activities will prove to you that you are capable of greatness. Once you've successfully accomplished several of them, examine the project that seems impossible. Write down all the small steps you need to do to achieve this goal, then start working on the first step. Continue working on each step, one at a time, until you've proven to yourself that this huge goal was not impossible and that you've achieved it.

Take time out to celebrate and reward yourself in some way. When you're ready, start work on the next challenge. By this time, you'll probably have discovered how much richer and exciting your life is when you're stretching your-self in this way. Your opportunities will multiply, and you'll receive your full share of all the good things life has to offer.

A former client of mine is a talented artist who loves painting and completely loses himself in his work. Twenty years ago, he was also painfully shy and sensitive. Conse-quently, he avoided exhibitions where his work might be criticized. He sold his work cheaply at markets for a frac-tion of what they should have been selling for. He came to me for help in gaining confidence after a customer bullied him into selling a painting for much less than the already low price he'd put on it. He wanted to be able to stand up for himself in that type of situation. During our prelim-inary discussion, he admitted that he had never sold his work in exhibitions or galleries due to his fear of criticism and rejection.

It took time before he felt brave enough to offer one of his works to a leading gallery. Fortunately, the art dealer was a kind man. He explained that my client needed to increase his prices by at *least* 300 percent! The painting sold quickly, and the dealer wanted more. Those works also sold, and people in art circles began talking about my client. It didn't take long until the dealer wanted to put on a solo exhibition of his works. Thinking of the criticism he might receive in the press, my client refused. Again, it took time before he overcame that fear, but he eventually agreed to do the exhibition. He did receive some criticism, but every single painting sold. In the space of twelve months, my client had changed from being a timid, scared man into a successful artist. Much to his surprise, the criticism didn't bother him—any negative comments were far outweighed by the accolades he received from the art collectors who bought his work. Today, his work is in many art museums around the world, and people have to be patient if they want to buy his work. If he hadn't been bullied into selling his work too cheaply twenty years ago, he might still be a struggling artist. At every step along the way, he's had to muster courage he didn't know he possessed. He richly deserves his success. I'm sure many struggling artists attribute his success to luck, and they're right. What they don't know is that he created his own luck by moving out of his comfort zone.

16

◆

Help Others

There's a famous Chinese proverb that says: "If you want happiness for an hour, take a nap. If you want happiness for a day, go fishing. If you want happiness for a month, get married. If you want happiness for a year, inherit a fortune. If you want happiness for a lifetime, help somebody else." Helping others is an altruistic act that has many benefits. It makes you feel good about yourself and the world, it improves the life of someone else, it connects you with another person, and your kindness may be passed on to others—philanthropy is contagious. It also changes the way you look at yourself. When you consciously seek opportunities to help others, you look at yourself differently and realize that you are a good person. You become aware that you are interconnected with everyone else.

Helping others doesn't necessarily mean donating money. You can help others in a variety of ways by being helpful, kind, and thoughtful. You might compliment a stranger. You could hold the door of an elevator open for someone, let a car in front of you on the freeway, or give up your seat on public transport to let an elderly person sit down. None of these costs anything but can make a great difference to the person you help.

You can help people in larger ways, too. You might buy a meal for a homeless person, check on an ill neighbor to make sure he or she is okay, donate to a good cause, volunteer your time and skill, or share your knowledge and expertise with others. A wonderful way to help others is to teach them useful skills that they'll be able to use to improve their lives.

Sometimes, the best way to help someone is simply to be there. You can provide company, listen, and offer conversation, as well as sympathy and a shoulder to lean on. Hugs, smiles, and kind words possess enormous power to help someone when they're in need. In *The Merchant of Venice*, William Shakespeare had Portia say: "How far that little candle throws his beams! So shines a good deed in a weary world" (Act 5, scene 1).

Some people help others without expecting or seeking any reward, in acts of total selflessness. Those who helped rescue the people trapped in the rubble of the twin towers in New York on September 11, 2001, didn't think of themselves before putting themselves in grave danger. They attempted to rescue people they didn't know but who desperately needed help. These people are true heroes.

Helping others automatically brings you good luck. Every time you help others, you also help yourself. As all good deeds are ultimately rewarded, your willingness to help others ensures that good things will happen to you. They may well come in the form of lucky opportunities.

17

✦

KEEP BUSY

There's a direct correlation to busyness and good luck. When I worked as a salesman, I regularly used a line attributed to Thomas A. Edison as an affirmation (see chapter 5). It was: "Everything comes to him who hustles while he waits" (Jones, 14). Of course, you need to be productive while you're "hustling," as most people complain about being too busy, even when they're not. You need to be efficient, and use your time wisely, to turn it into luck.

Lucky people earn their good luck by working hard to achieve their goals. When the right opportunity reveals itself, they're prepared and ready to do whatever it takes to make it a success.

Being busy in itself is neither good nor bad, unless you're affecting your health and relationships by overworking. However, many people think that the word "busy" equates to being important, successful, or good. This might

be why so many people respond to "How are you?" by saying they're busy. It's all very well to be busy if there's a need
to be, but you must allow enough time to relax and rest. The
Japanese even have a word—*karoshi*—to describe people
who die of overwork.

Being constantly busy doesn't necessarily mean that
you're being productive. To make the most of your time,
you need to be well organized and have a plan of action.
Many people fail at the preparation stage, as they're in too
much of a hurry to get started. Could you create a system
to make the task easier? Ideally, you should do one thing at
a time. Multitasking only works when you're doing mind-
less or unimportant tasks. Have you ever watched someone
walk along the sidewalk while texting? They can't walk in
a straight line, and they're oblivious to everything around
them—a potentially dangerous combination. You should
also ask if it's necessary to do this particular task. Does it
help you reach one of your goals?

It is very important to set aside a certain amount of
time for rest. It may sound strange, but you're likely to finish the task more quickly and effectively if you take a short
break every hour or so. I spend most of my working time
sitting at a computer. For the last few years, I've been getting up every fifty minutes and walking around the house
or garden for five to ten minutes before returning to sit
down. I may or may not think about what I'm working on

during this brief break. However, I always return to my desk feeling refreshed and ready to work again.

Being busy can provide lucky opportunities but you need to live a full, well-balanced life. If you constantly feel overworked and too busy, you'll miss much of the joy in life. It might be helpful to learn how to delegate and say no. You might need to learn how to prioritize tasks related to your work.

Another problem might be the way in which you perceive busyness. Being busy is supposed to be good. People tend to view busy people as hardworking, productive achievers. However, this may not actually be the case. The busy person might be going around in circles achieving nothing, while another colleague is working half as hard and producing good results. We're all allocated twenty-four hours a day, and it's important to spend those hours wisely. You might have to let go of things in your life that are draining you of energy and holding you back or have otherwise outworn their use to create time for the tasks that you consider meaningful and important. You won't attract luck if you constantly feel as though you're on a treadmill. Dolly Parton said: "Don't get so busy making a living that you forget to make a life" (*Harper's Bazaar* January, 2018).

Genuinely busy people attract luck to them. This is because they're constantly being exposed to new ideas, and need to find ways to use everything they learn in the most effective way they can. They're also often involved in activities outside their work that can provide opportunities they can capitalize on.

An acquaintance of mine volunteered to help at a charity that provided meals for homeless people. He quickly discovered better and more efficient ways that the charity could use to prepare and distribute their meals. A year or two later, he started a catering company, utilizing many of the ideas he'd learned and created while helping out in the community. He's still running this business twenty years later, and has always donated a percentage of his profits to the charity that helped him discover a new career.

18

◆

LISTEN

One of Ernest Hemingway's best-known quotes is: "When people talk, listen carefully. Most people never listen" (Cowley, 90). Most people would rather hear themselves talk than listen to what someone else has to say. If you're wanting to learn, it's not hard to find someone who enjoys talking who will be delighted to find someone who's prepared to listen. If you're genuinely interested in what a person has to say, listen carefully, ask questions, and pay attention to the answers you receive, you'll learn a great deal. Sooner or later, you'll learn information that you can turn to your advantage. You can learn from anyone if you ask the right open-ended questions.

Most people need little encouragement to continue talking, but you still need to show that you're paying attention. Look the person in the eye about 60 to 70 percent of the time, using a relaxed gaze, and use your body language and facial expressions to express interest. Every now and again, nod your head in agreement, smile, and repeat or rephrase something that's been said. When the person stops talking, resist the temptation to immediately tell a story involving you. Instead, ask questions about what you've just heard. This tells the person that you're thinking about what he or she told you and are interested in learning more.

There's a big difference between hearing and listening. Hearing is a passive process that involves processing sounds in the brain. We hear traffic noises, or the sound of children at play. Listening, however, is a conscious action. To listen, you need to pay attention to the words that are being said. At the same time, you need to be aware of the speaker's body language, emotional state, and intensity.

Chances are that you've never been taught how to listen. It's a skill, and like any other skill, it can be learned. Practice listening, really listening to every word, and don't plan your response until the person has finished speaking. This tells the person that what they're saying is important. Most people think of their response while the other person is still talking. This means that they fail to hear much of what the other person is saying. Don't jump in before the other person has finished speaking. In addition to appearing rude, it also shows that you're not listening properly.

Naturally, not every conversation will be scintillating and informative. Over the years, you've likely endured many seemingly endless boring conversations about things that don't interest you or are unimportant and don't matter. You certainly could handle these conversations by scrolling through Facebook while the person is talking or letting your eyes glaze over, but these solutions are unkind. A better idea is to realize that the person simply needs to be heard. Ask a few questions and listen until you have an opportunity to end the conversation without causing offence.

British politican and author Sir Winston Churchill (1874–1965) was fascinated with the concept of luck, and during his long life he was the recipient of many examples of good luck. His curiosity and ability to listen enabled him to produce a magician to entertain the troops during the Boer War. He and several other war correspondents happened to ride past a line of Boer prisoners and saw one expertly knotting a bandage on his left arm with his right hand. The other correspondents continued riding, but Churchill was intrigued and stopped to speak to the prisoner, who fortunately spoke good English. He told Churchill that before the war he was a German magician who made his living performing sleight of hand in music halls.

A day or two later, Churchill heard the British commander talking about the low morale of his bored men. Churchill immediately suggested that a professional magic show would entertain everyone. No one took him seriously, but he produced the magician who gave an excellent show. To show his appreciation, the general gave Churchill a previously unknown piece of news that became a scoop for his newspaper. If Churchill hadn't stopped and listened to the German magician, the troops would not have been entertained, and Churchill would not have had his scoop. It's not surprising that Sir Winston Churchill was often referred to as "that lucky devil, Churchill" (Carr, 25–26).

Larry King, the American talk show host, once said: "I remind myself every morning: Nothing I say this day will teach me anything. So, if I'm going to learn, I must do it by listening." If you take an active interest in everyone you encounter, and then listen actively, you'll learn a great deal, and may well become a "lucky devil."

19

◆

Seize Opportunities

Opportunities are everywhere. I used to know a man who found several opportunities every morning while reading the daily newspaper. He looked for items he could buy and resell quickly, often within hours of having bought them. On one occasion I visited him and his back yard was full of metal shelving. He sold it by making one phone call and then went off to buy something else. I met him when we bought a lifetime's supply of blankets after he'd purchased a warehouse full of them. After that, I regularly received phone calls from him whenever he'd obtained something he thought might interest me. He was an extremely wealthy man when he died. I'm sure if he was alive today, he'd do most of his business online and would be even richer than he was in those pre-internet days.

The opportunities that he discovered on a daily basis were available to everyone, but somehow, he was able to see things that other people overlooked. He attributed his success entirely to luck, but I think there's much more to it than that.

The first step is to put aside your doubts and fears and start looking for opportunities. You do this by being curious and asking questions. There could be a good opportunity whenever you ask a question that no one seems able to answer. Problems are surprisingly useful in this process, as they provide opportunities to learn and grow.

Decide on the types of opportunities you're looking for. You might be searching for a good business idea or a romantic relationship. You might want to buy a reliable car for a good price. Knowing what you want is an essential part of the process.

You also need to recognize the opportunity when it appears. It may appear in the form of a problem, or involve a great deal of hard work. Opportunities are seldom handed to you on a silver plate.

Say yes whenever a good opportunity appears. Naturally, you must evaluate the opportunity first, but if it looks promising, don't delay too long—someone else might seize it while you're still thinking about it.

Opportunities always involve risk. Uncertainty is a fact of life, and we're surrounded by risks every day. Even crossing a quiet street involves a certain degree of risk. Some people, such as extreme athletes, embrace risk, while others will do anything to avoid it. Ask yourself if you're prepared to take the risk that the opportunity may not work out the way you wanted. Act only if your answer is yes. If the opportunity you're exploring looks as if it will cause you too much stress and worry, and sleepless nights, it might be better to let it go and search for another opportunity.

A friend of mine has an engraved message on his desk that says: "Luck is recognizing an opportunity when it appears and being brave enough to reach out and take it." You sometimes need to be brave to make the most of lucky opportunities. Fear, doubt, and worry hold many people back and prevent them from taking the vital first step toward success.

20

◆

Set Goals and Achieve Them

We all daydream about what we'd like to do, have, or become. For most people, these remain nothing but idle thoughts, but some are able to turn their dreams into goals and make them happen. Goals provide focus and direction. My first boss when I left school told me: "Successful people set goals, failures don't." He explained that goal-setters achieve more in life as they know where they're going. Setting a goal for yourself is also extremely motivating.

Setting goals works, and in recent years there has been a great deal of research into how effective it can be. As I have two grandsons at college, I was particularly interested in a study that showed that setting goals and acting on them improved academic success (Morisano et al., 2010).

Your goal needs to be as specific as possible. It's not enough, for instance, to set a goal of earning more money. If that is your goal, decide exactly how much money you want to earn. You also need a deadline. Once you've decided on the specific amount of money you want, you need to decide when you will have it. You also need to determine what you're going to do to earn the amount of money you desire.

The first step to setting a goal is to make sure that it's something you really want to achieve. It needs to be something that excites and motivates you. It is, ideally, something that requires time, persistence, and commitment. There's no point in putting time and effort into something that's not of great importance to you, as you're likely to give up at the first sign of difficulty. Even if you succeed, it will provide little satisfaction. Recently, I met a man who became a doctor to satisfy his parent's expectations. He never practiced medicine, though—he now works as a property developer.

Your goals need to be challenging but not impossible. There's no point in setting a goal that you know is impossible for you. I could, for instance, set a goal of winning an Olympic gold medal. However, at my age, that would be completely unrealistic. In fact, it would have been unrealistic at any age, as I was never motivated to excel at any sport.

Write your goal on a card and carry it with you. This means you can read it whenever you have a spare moment during the day. You should also read it when you first get up in the morning, and immediately before going to bed at night. This encourages your subconscious mind to come up with ideas to help you reach your goal. The point of writing your goal is that it represents an agreement you make with yourself. If it's not written down, sooner or later, you're likely to forget it. However, if you carry it with you, and see it several times a day, you won't be able to quietly forget about it.

The next step is to create two lists. The first itemizes all the benefits you'll receive as a result of achieving this goal. You can add additional items to this list whenever you think of them. This list will help keep you motivated when progress is harder or slower than you had hoped. You should read this list every day and visualize yourself reaching your goal. Make it as vivid as possible: add emotion and as many senses as are relevant to make it feel real.

The second list is just as important as the first one. It's a detailed listing of everything you need to do to achieve your goal. Each step should be as small and as achievable as possible. Each step brings you closer to your goal. Write the deadline you have for each step beside it. This will keep you on track and keep you motivated to do something every day. Cross off each step as you achieve it. This alone can be extremely satisfying and motivating.

You can set yourself as many goals as you wish. Set some small goals that you can achieve relatively easily, and also set some more demanding long-term goals. You might even have a lifetime goal that you can work on. You might decide to set goals that relate to your home and family, career, finances, physical fitness, self-development, hobbies and interests, and your community.

Celebrate each time you achieve a goal or make worthwhile progress on a long-term goal. When I'm writing a book, I reward myself at different stages. I might take my wife out for dinner or a movie after finishing a particular chapter, for instance. The prospect of an evening out keeps me motivated, and I try to beat my self-imposed deadline by a day or two.

The famous Spanish artist Pablo Picasso (1881–1973) said: "Our goals can only be reached through a vehicle of a plan, in which we must fervently believe, and upon which we must vigorously act" (https://www.pablopicasso.org/quotes.jsp). Setting a goal involves making a plan, and setting goals for yourself will make you luckier. You'll know where you're going and how you're going to get there. You'll gain confidence in your ability to achieve anything you set your mind on. You'll be motivated to achieve your goals and will discover what you want to achieve in life.

Here's how you can decide whether or not a goal is worth pursuing:

1. Evaluate the situation. Think about whatever it is you want to achieve, and ask yourself how much time and effort you're willing to put in to achieve this goal. You should also ask if you're prepared to work hard on this project and persist until you've achieved it.

2. You should also ask yourself why you want to achieve this goal. Think about the rewards you'll receive as a result of achieving it. You must have at least one significant benefit that will make all the hard work worthwhile. If the rewards are worthwhile, you'll need to keep focused on them while you start working on your goal.

3. Write down a list of all the steps you'll need to take to achieve your goal. Ensure that each step is achievable in a reasonable length of time. People often give up when the ultimate goal seems far away or overwhelming. This won't occur if you focus on each small step.

4. Evaluate the situation again. If you're happy and prepared to pay the price, start working on the first step to achieving the goal. If you have doubts, go through the steps again, and then ask yourself if you're prepared to pay the price. Proceed only when you're 100 percent certain that this goal is something that you have to achieve.

21

◆

Visualization

Visualization is the ability to consciously imagine what you want. Walt Disney created Disneyland in his mind after watching his daughters playing and imagining a place where adults and children of all ages could have fun together. Despite difficulties in raising the money and plenty of skepticism, Walt Disney was determined to make his dream a reality. With the help of a team of supportive people who believed in his vision, Disneyland opened in Anaheim, California, in 1955. He called the process of visualization "Imagineering," and the Disney theme park designers are still called imagineers today.

You're already a good visualizer. You visualize every time you daydream, think of someone you know, or remember an incident from the past. Visualization can be used in many ways, such as therapy, healing, pain control, and self-improvement. It can also be used to attract good luck.

With practice, you'll be able to consciously visualize wherever you happen to be. Initially, though, the best place to start visualization is to lie on your back with your hands and feet uncrossed. Use whatever is necessary to make yourself comfortable. You might like to use a pillow and a blanket. Loosen any clothing that feels tight.

Close your eyes and relax as much as you can. Take three or four slow, deep breaths and say the word "relax" to yourself each time you exhale. After that, allow the muscles in your toes and feet to relax, and slowly work your way up your body to the top of your head, letting go of any tension and relaxing each muscle along the way. It's an enjoyable process and there's no need to rush it. Take as long as is necessary to ensure that your whole body is completely relaxed.

Once you feel fully relaxed, focus on your particular desire or goal. If you haven't worked out what it is you want, think about the home you grew up in as a child. See it as clearly as you can in your mind's eye. See the property from the outside, and then walk through the house, "seeing" each room in your mind as you do so. Some people are able to "see" things clearly when they visualize, almost as if they're actually looking at whatever it happens to be. Some people see things less clearly, while others experience the visualization using other senses such as sound, taste, and feeling. It doesn't matter how you experience visualization. With practice, your ability to see or sense during a visualization will improve.

You can make the experience feel more real by adding tastc, hearing, smell, touch, and movement to the visualization. Add emotion, if you can.

Enjoy the visualization for as long as you wish. When you feel ready, silently count from one to five, open your eyes, stretch, and spend a minute or two thinking about the experience.

Once you've done this a few times, think of a specific goal or desire you have and repeat the visualization using it as the focus of the exercise. Think of your desire using as much emotion and feeling as you can. See yourself once you've attained your goal—see how thrilled and happy you are. The mind cannot tell the difference between an actual experience and a thought that has been vividly imagined. Consequently, you will ultimately achieve your goal if you believe with all your heart that you will achieve it, repeat the visualization regularly, and do whatever work is required.

One of the most useful ways to visualize is to think about your future. Where will you be five years from now? You want your visualization to reveal the life you want to be living. Consequently, visualize, fantasize, and "see" yourself five years from now. See yourself having fun with family and friends. See the pleasant environment, the beautiful car you'll be driving, the satisfying work you'll be doing, and the lifestyle you'll be enjoying. Make the picture as clear as you can. Allow yourself to feel excited that this amazing life will be yours in just five years. You'll probably be surprised at some of the pictures that come into your mind. Don't judge or censor anything. It simply means that your subconscious mind is adding detail to your visualization. Consequently, you should follow the crazier ideas that come into your mind and see where they go. They might lead you to a future life that goes well beyond your current hopes and dreams.

Repeat the visualization every day, if possible. It will be slightly different every time you do it. Believe with every fiber of your being that this is the future you're going to have. With constant repetition, your mind will act on the visualization and make it happen.

However, it won't happen without effort on your part. After each visualization, you'll need to make notes about what you saw and experienced and turn it all into workable goals. If you do this and follow through by acting on your goals, your seemingly impossible dream will become a reality.

In his classic book, *Think and Grow Rich*, Napoleon Hill wrote about a visualization he did for many years to develop his character. In his visualization, he saw himself chairing a meeting with nine men he wanted to emulate: Ralph Waldo Emerson, Thomas Paine, Thomas Edison, Charles Darwin, Abraham Lincoln, Luther Burbank, Napoleon Bonaparte, Henry Ford, and Andrew Carnegie. During his visualizations, he asked these famous men for information that would enable him to become a composite of all the most positive aspects of their characters. Even though Napoleon Hill was always aware that they were imaginary, the visualizations helped him develop his character and put him on the path to success (Hill, 215–218).

Approach all your visualization sessions with a positive attitude and a curious mind. Visualization and goal setting is an incredibly powerful combination that will enable you to achieve your dreams and become as lucky as you want to be.

22

❖

CREATIVITY

Creativity is the ability to use your imagination to create original and different ideas, and to then act on
them to make them real. The finished result can be intangible or physical. Everyone has an imagination, giving them
the ability to come up with ideas. However, people are not
considered to be creative unless they act on them. People
who don't act on their ideas are considered to be imaginative, rather than creative. Fortunately, we all have the ability
to be creative.

American psychologist Abraham Maslow (1908–1970)
wrote that "a first-rate soup is more creative than a second-
rate painting, and that, generally, cooking or parenthood or
making a home could be creative while poetry need not be;
it could be uncreative" (Maslow, 22). He meant that creativity can be applied to almost anything and is not something
available only to artistic people. To create good luck in your

life, you need to use your innate creativity to produce ideas that are useful to you. And before you can do this, you need to have a problem that needs to be solved. Write whatever it is at the top of a sheet of paper. You might, for instance, write:

> I want to write a poem.

> I want to ask my boss for a pay rise.

> I want to bake a fruit cake.

> My daughter and I are arguing all the time.

Look at the sentence you wrote and ask yourself as many questions about it as you can, starting with the words who, what, where, when, why, and how. Write these questions down, and include any solutions that come into your mind while you're doing this exercise.

If possible, perform a visualization involving the problem and some of the questions. See what comes into your mind. After you've done this, switch the scene so that you're now looking at the situation once the problem's been resolved: you've written the poem, asked for the pay rise, or whatever your goal was, and achieved the result you wanted. Allow yourself to feel a sense of happiness and satisfaction now that the problem has been resolved. From this vantage point, look back and visualize the steps you took to achieve the desired result. When you've completed the visualization, write down all the insights that came to you while you were doing it.

You now have a wealth of information to work with. Read everything you've written about the problem and follow it with writing a list of potential solutions. Write these solutions as quickly as you can—the important thing is to record every possible solution, no matter how strange or outlandish it might seem. It's difficult to be creative when you're analyzing and criticizing your ideas at the same time. Remember that something that seems ridiculous at first sight might ultimately lead you to the perfect solution.

If other people are involved, such as in the "my daughter and I are arguing" problem, perform a visualization in which you reverse roles. Start by explaining the problem from your point of view, and then see it through the eyes and mind of the other person or people involved. You may find a solution, or an effective compromise. Again, write everything down as soon as you can afterward.

One creative method I frequently use for problem-solving is to visualize a long hotel hallway. There are doors lining both walls, and behind each one is a solution to the problem. Each door is painted differently. Visualize yourself walking along the hallway and stopping outside a door that appeals to you. Open the door, and walk into a scene that helps you resolve the problem. If you're writing a poem, there might be someone inside the room who says the first line to you. If you're asking your boss for a pay rise, you might see him sitting behind his desk.

There are two chairs facing him, and sitting on one of them is an expert on negotiation. He or she tells you exactly what to say. Visualize the look on your boss's face as he realizes that you're worthy of a good pay rise. See him offering it to you and feel a sense of joy and happiness as you accept it.

You can open as many doors as you wish and enter different scenes with different solutions in each one.

By the time you've completed this, you should have at least a dozen potential solutions to your problem. Now it's time to start thinking logically again. Analyze each solution and see if you can improve it in any way. You might be able to combine two or more solutions, for instance. You might discard some of them until you have one or two, maybe more, that you believe you can develop. Once you've used your creativity to reach this stage, you'll be ready to set goals and create an action plan to make your idea a reality.

23

◆

Choose Your Friends Wisely

I vividly remember my mother telling me not to associate with some of my classmates as they were "a bad influence." I had no idea what she meant at the time; some of them were friends and I enjoyed spending time with them. However, it turned out that she was correct—those friends all got into trouble of one sort or another as they grew up. My parents knew that the company one keeps has a strong influence for good or bad. To lead a happy and successful life, it's important to associate with good and honest people.

It's possible to predict how successful you'll be five years from now by looking at your friends. They clearly reveal the sort of work you'll be doing, how much you'll be earning, and your overall satisfaction with life. If your friends are all people who don't have much motivation and haven't done much with their lives, what does that say about you?

An old saying says that you become like the five people you spend most time with. If this is true, your life will obviously be completely different if your friends are motivated and ambitious than it will be if they're lazy and unmotivated. A friend of mine has a poster on his home office wall that says: "If your friends don't motivate and inspire you, you're choosing them all wrong."

You want friends who are honest and supportive. These friends may sometimes tell you things that you don't want to hear, but they'll be doing it for the right reasons, and in time you'll appreciate them for that. You'll be able to share your goals and dreams with these friends and know that they'll encourage you to achieve them. They'll also be the first to congratulate you when you reach them. Likewise, choose friends who can see potential in you that you may not even be aware of yourself.

Your friends should stimulate, motivate, and encourage you. Positive people are fun to be with. Negative people drag you down to their level and drain you of motivation and energy. Good friends bring out the best in you.

You need friends you can laugh with. These friends will appreciate you for who you are and will love your quirks and strange habits.

True friends will stand by you during difficult times. "Fair weather" friends disappear as soon as the going gets tough. Everyone has ups and downs in their lives, and true friends offer a shoulder to lean on and a hand to hold during the tough times.

Choose friends with similar interests to you. This gives you plenty to talk about, as well as different events you can attend, and different activities you can participate in together.

Choose friends who give as much as they take. One-sided relationships in which one person constantly takes almost always end badly. Be willing to compromise. Sometimes you might take part in something your friend wants to do instead of something you'd rather to be doing, while at other times your friend will go along with your desires instead of their own. Friendships should be mutually supportive.

To find a friend, be a friend. You can meet like-minded people by taking classes or joining clubs. Volunteering is another good way to meet potential friends. I met one of my best friends when I sold him a hot dog to raise funds for a children's charity. I've also made friends with some of the people I worked with at that charity. One of my sons is keen on sports and always talks to the people sitting beside him at football games. As a result, he's made many friends.

A study conducted by the Centre for Aging Studies at Flinders University in Adelaide, Australia, followed nearly fifteen hundred people aged seventy years or older for ten years. They found that people with a large network of friends outlived those with fewer friends by 22 percent. The authors of the study concluded that the reason for this is because good friends discourage negative activities such as smoking and excess drinking. The companionship of friends increases self-esteem, provides support when necessary, and decreases depression. As older people become more selective in their friendships, they choose to spend most of their time with people they genuinely like. Interestingly, close relationships with children, other relatives, and a spouse had little effect on longevity (https://jech.bmj.com/content/59/7/574).

Everyone finds that friends come and go all throughout life. Life changes such as marriage, divorce, moving to another city, having children, and a change in career, all affect friendships in different ways. Some people get so busy in their own lives that they have no time for friends. This is not a good thing to do because it's essential for your health and length of life—and of course your happiness—that you make time for friends. One of the best ways to come up with lucky ideas is while you're having fun with friends. This enables you to discuss ideas in a relaxed, casual situation without stress or pressure.

Because your choice of friends affects everything you do, it's vital that you choose them carefully. Here are some thoughts to keep in mind:

1. Make friends with people who have big goals and a strong sense of purpose.

2. Choose supportive friends who will cheer you on and enjoy your successes.

3. Choose friends who are optimistic, positive, and motivating.

4. Make friends with people who are heading in the same direction as you but may be slightly older and perhaps a few steps ahead.

5. Make friends with people who have similar interests to you.

6. Make friends with people who are curious about life and enjoy learning.

7. Be the best friend you can be in return.

24

◆

Use Open Body Language

Imagine you're at a party and speak to a number of people during the course of the evening. Two people in particular stand out in your memory: one looked over your shoulder while you were talking and hardly made eye contact, and the other made good eye contact, smiled frequently, nodded from time to time as you talked, and used their hands while speaking to you. Which of these people is interested in you? The first person was looking over your shoulder to see if they could find someone more interesting to talk to, while the second person was obviously enjoying the conversation you were having. Chances are that neither of them was aware of what their body language was telling you, but only the second person was also using open body language.

Open body language means that the person is open and receptive to you and interested in continuing the conversation. It also means that the body is open—arms and legs are uncrossed, leaving the torso exposed. Someone with open body language will be looking directly at you with relaxed eyes and a gentle gaze. The person will look into your eyes some of the time, looking away every now and again. Scientists have found that if you're talking to a stranger, eye contact should last for about 3.2 seconds at a time. People tend to feel intimidated if someone stares directly into their eyes for long periods of time. (https://www.scientificamerican.com/article/eye-contact-how-long-is-too-long/) Usually, the person who is listening will look at the speaker's eyes between 60 to 70 percent of the time and the speaker will make eye contact about 40 percent of the time.

The person will also smile, nod in agreement, and make other gestures to demonstrate that they are paying attention. They will face toward you and the hands will be open with the palms exposed. Although the person may use his or her arms expressively, most of the time the torso will be exposed.

The legs will be uncrossed, and slightly apart. The person's feet will point toward you, showing interest in you. The position of a person's feet indicates what they want to do. If they want to end the conversation or leave the room, their feet will likely to point toward the door. It's also possible to display an open posture while sitting down. Sit upright and avoid slouching.

When your body is open like this, you'll find you're receptive and positive about your interaction with the other person. Your body assumes this position naturally when you're chatting with a good friend or are feeling relaxed and confident in the environment you're in. Fortunately, you can adopt this position whenever you wish, and you'll become aware of positive, open feelings in your body.

You don't need to do this consciously, either. If you imagine that the person you're talking to is a good friend, the open body language will look after itself.

The old saying that you never get a second chance to make a good first impression is true, as people start making their minds up about people they meet in a matter of seconds. In the 1980s, Dr. Michael R. Solomon, a social psychologist and marketing expert, conducted research at the Graduate School of Business in New York. His findings suggest that we make eleven decisions about someone we've just met in the first seven seconds. They are the person's economic level, educational level and intelligence, honesty and credibility, trustworthiness, level of sophistication, gender and sexual orientation, level of success, political background, values and principles, ethnic background, and social desirability. If you want people to immediately see you as someone who is friendly and approachable, you need to use open body language.

People are reluctant to change their opinion of someone once they've made it. This may not seem fair—after all, no one is at their best all the time. However, failing to make a good first impression can be expensive.

Many years ago, a bread shop opened up close to our home. I was excited at the thought of being able to buy a variety of breads within easy walking distance of our house. I could smell the aroma of freshly baked bread as I walked along the street. When I went in, the bread was attractively presented and displayed. There was no one behind the counter, so I pressed the bell. I could hear someone out the back but whoever it was didn't respond. I pressed the bell again, and nothing happened. Finally, I called out, "Hello!" A man in his midthirties appeared. He snarled at me and said, "Whaddaya want?" I stared at him for several seconds, then turned around and returned home. I assumed the man had been busy doing some task out back and was annoyed at the interruption, but I never found out what he was doing. I never went inside his shop again.

Using open body language also increases your opportunities for attracting good luck, as you'll meet many more people, some of whom will expose you to new ideas and opportunities.

25

◆

Expect the
Unexpected

Expecting the unexpected means that anything might
happen and probably will. Change is inevitable, and
you must be prepared to deal with anything that you hav-
en't anticipated. There are plenty of opportunities waiting
for people who're willing to take advantage of changes that
might occur. If you see only the things you expect to see,
you'll miss out on these potentially lucky opportunities.

I used to work with someone who worried when
everything was going well; he was convinced the situation
wouldn't last. He was right of course, as the only constant in
life is change. However, he was foolish in worrying during
the good times because he failed to experience the joy and
happiness that occurs when everything in life is going well.

A death in the family, an accident, the loss of a job, a
divorce, or a natural disaster can unexpectedly hit at any

time, and the manner in which the changed situation is dealt with can reveal much about a person's character and resilience. Forethought can partially resolve the difficulties caused by catastrophes such as these. Insurance can cover the costs of some of them, for instance, and a good support network of friends and family can ease the grief of others. Unexpected events such as these can dramatically change people's lives in a split second. People who are naturally optimistic usually fare better than pessimists in this type of situation, as they immediately start thinking of what they can do to make the best of the current situation.

Murphy's Law states that if anything can go wrong, it will. I was surprised to learn that Captain Edward Aloysius Murphy Jr. (1918–1990) was a real person. He was an American aerospace engineer who worked on safety-critical systems for the US Air Force. According to an engineer who was present at the time, Murphy apparently blamed an assistant for the failure of an experiment by saying, "If that guy has any way of making a mistake, he will" (Dickson, 128–137).

Another way of looking at "expect the unexpected" is to anticipate the possibilities of events occurring before they actually do, a perspective which puts you in control. Like millions of other commuters around the world, my granddaughter drives to and from work during rush hour. She usually avoids the freeway due to the high probability of it being gridlocked. She also listens to radio traffic reports before choosing the best way to get home. By doing this, she is seldom surprised by unexpected events.

Anticipating what could go wrong before starting on a project will save time in the long run, though Murphy's Law still applies. My neighbor is an airplane engineer, and it is his company's policy to detail everything that could go wrong before starting any major work. He tells me that often they'd detail absolutely everything except for one possibility…and that was always the one thing that went wrong.

Obviously you'll know what to do if the unexpected occurrence is a positive one, but it can be difficult to know what to do when something negative happens unexpectedly. Here are some suggestions:

1. Keep in control. Take several slow, deep breaths before reacting. Remember that your attitude about the situation is important. If you remain as positive as you can, you'll retain control rather than allowing the circumstance to have control over you.

2. Avoid anger or self-pity. Remember that unexpected situations happen to everyone. Although it's frustrating and may make life difficult for a while, you will get over it.

3. Work out what you need to do to resolve the situation. It might be helpful to write a plan of the actions you need to take, the people you need to

contact, and how much money it might cost. If you know anyone who has been through a similar experience, contact them and ask for their suggestions and advice.

4. Take whatever actions are required to resolve the situation.

26

❖

Take
Calculated Risks

A calculated risk is something that is undertaken after considering the likelihood of success. There is a chance of failure in attempting anything risky, and consequently the probability of failure needs to be estimated before starting whatever it happens to be. General George S. Patton (1885–1945) said: "Take calculated risks. That is quite different from being rash." Lucky people take calculated risks. People who aren't prepared to leave anything to chance won't make many mistakes, but they won't achieve much either.

Naturally, it is best to minimize the risk and avoid doing anything dangerous or foolhardy. Fortunately, most risks are not life-threatening; when you think about it, almost every decision you make is potentially risky. You take a risk every time you make the first move and introduce yourself to a stranger at a party. You take a risk when you ask for a pay rise. You might be rebuffed when you introduce yourself to someone, but that person might also become a good friend. You could get turned down when you ask for a pay rise but might receive a bigger pay rise than you expected.

A friend of mine often talks about the day he got turned down when he asked for a pay rise. He told just one person about what happened and added that he might look for a better job. The person he told the story to offered him a job on the spot. It seemed like a huge risk—the person offering had a one-man locksmith business, and there was no guarantee of enough work for two people. Though my friend's wife wanted him to stay where he was, he accepted the job offer after thinking it through. A few years later, he was offered a partnership in the business and is now a successful businessman. What might have initially seemed like an unlucky day turned out to be the luckiest day of his life.

My friend accepted the job offer based on his opinion of the man who'd offered him the job. He'd known the man for several years and knew that he was a hard worker who had a good reputation. He asked mutual acquaintances about him, and everyone spoke highly of him. Because of that, he considered the risk worth taking, and events proved him right.

Here are some ideas to think about before making a calculated risk:

1. Evaluate the risk as logically as possible. Determine if the proposed risk is in keeping with your aims and objectives.

2. Be willing to say no. You can't say yes to everything. Consequently, you may have to turn down some good opportunities while waiting for the right one to appear. Naturally, it is also wise to say no if the opportunity appears to entail too great a risk.

3. Do as much research as you can before proceeding. Consider every possible outcome that could occur, positive and negative. You'll probably focus mainly on the positive, and the result might be better than you'd anticipated. However, it's always a good idea to look at the potential negative outcomes, too. What would you do if the risk didn't work out? Think about everything that could possibly go wrong. Would you be able to change course and rescue the situation? How would you feel if you had no other option than to walk away to cut your losses? Examine every possible scenario before making a decision.

4. Have regular checkpoints. These are times when you pause and make sure that everything is going according to plan. Ideally, you'll have set a number of smaller goals to help you on the way to achieving your main goal. These provide convenient times

to check on how well—or badly—your project is
going.

5. Be willing to change or adapt quickly if the project
doesn't go according to plan, and becomes too risky.

Many people fear any form of risk, forgetting that
they've taken many risks already in their lives. Learning
to walk was probably the first major one, and learning to
swim or drive are just two more. You should obviously say
no to any risks that strike you as foolish, but think carefully
before turning down a calculated risk that stacks up.

In New Zealand, everyone over the age of eighty needs
a medical certificate every two years to retain their driver's
license. An elderly client of mine has been driving without a valid license for five years, as she's certain it would
not be renewed because of her bad eyesight. Her blind son
lives with her, so she says she needs her license to drive him
wherever he needs to go. However, she'll be caught sooner
or later; if that happens, she'll lose her license permanently.
Is she taking a foolish or a calculated risk?

27

◆

Adaptability

A quote often attributed to Charles Darwin says: "The most important factor in survival is neither intelligence nor strength but adaptability." This quote was actually written by Professor Leon C. Megginson, who paraphrased Darwin's work in a single sentence that was published in the *Southwestern Social Sciences Quarterly* in 1963 (44(1): 3–13). No matter who wrote it, the writer was saying that the ability to adjust to a situation is more important than intellect and power. Someone who is adaptable can quickly change or adjust his or her course, actions, or approach when the situation demands it. A friend of mine owned an office building. During a time of economic downturn, his tenant left and he couldn't find anyone prepared to lease it. He turned the building into serviced offices and meeting rooms and ended up getting a greater return for his investment than he would have received if he'd managed to lease it. A newspaper article described him as an entrepreneur who knew how to turn lemons into lemonade.

I also knew two people who owned a company that made carbon paper. It was successful for many years, but they were too slow to adapt when times changed. As photocopying and carbonless copying paper reduced the need for carbon paper, they struggled; the quick growth of computers and word processing proved to be the final nail in the coffin. Their failure to adapt proved to be an expensive lesson.

Adaptable people are alert to any changes that occur in their business or environment. If you're manufacturing a product that is declining in popularity, for instance, you need to start improving or making changes to it, or look for other products you can produce and sell to replace it.

Adaptable people are also constantly learning new skills. They know that changes invariably occur and it is therefore important to keep up-to-date with what's going on in their market. They read books and articles, attend classes and courses, and do anything else that's necessary to keep them informed. Of course, when they take advantage of this knowledge, people say they're "lucky."

Adaptability is an important skill for leaders and entrepreneurs. These roles require people who are flexible, inquisitive, embracing of change, willing to experiment and try anything new, and plan ahead. These skills are especially vital in today's world with new innovations and rapidly evolving technology changing our lives on a regular basis. Think of the changes that have taken place in telephones, computers, television, music, publishing, banking, and education over the last twenty-five years.

Businesses must change and adapt to move forward. Some huge companies, such as Pan Am and Bethlehem Steel, failed to adapt and are no longer in business. Other corporations are famous for their ability to change and adapt. A striking example of this is Nokia, the Finnish multinational corporation. It began in 1865 as a pulp and paper company, and thirty-five years later became a power generating company. It gradually moved into telephone equipment, rubber, plastic, television, and computers. In time, the company became interested in electronics and radio, and the opportunities they saw in these fields encouraged them to move into mobile communications. They divested their interests in other businesses and today are one of the world's leading companies in telecommunications technology.

The ability to adapt to changing circumstances is just as important in everyday life. The ability to adapt and bounce back after a traumatic event is called emotional resilience. Everyone experiences ups and downs in life, but adaptable people are able to adjust and regain their equilibrium quickly. They're lucky, as this ability is also a strong indicator of longevity (Chopra, 18).

28

❖

Change One
Thing

If you could change one thing about yourself or your life, what would it be? Would you choose to exercise more, eat less, or be more assertive or maybe more loving? It doesn't matter how many things you want to change, but to increase your luck you need to make just one change at a time. If you try to do too many simultaneously, you won't succeed at any of them. Change is never easy and becomes impossible if you want to overcome a sugar addiction, exercise more, learn computer programming, take up chess, overcome shyness, and reduce stress all at the same time. However, you could do all of these if you tackled them one after the other.

Once you've decided what you want to change, you need to decide exactly how, where, and when you'll do whatever is necessary to make the change. If you want to improve your fitness, for instance, you might join a gym, hire a personal trainer, and exercise four times every week.

You need to keep your ultimate goal in mind. Write it down as an affirmation and carry it with you. When you wake up in the morning, take a few moments to visualize yourself five or ten years from now as the person you'll be once the change has been made. Some people focus solely on their goal, but you'll have better results if you enjoy the process of achieving it.

It takes at least twenty-eight days for a habit change to occur, so allow about two months before making another one. By that time, you should be doing everything necessary to achieve your first habit change, and it should be a normal part of your everyday life. If this is the case, you'll continue doing it while starting to make the next change.

You'll find that one successful change is likely to favorably affect all the other changes you want to make. If the first change was to stop drinking half a bottle of wine every night, you'll find that achieving that will also help you lose the weight you want to lose. It will make you feel better, which might in turn encourage you to go to the gym. If you don't drink in the evening, you'll have sufficient energy and time to learn a foreign language, take up art, catch up with friends, read a good book, or do anything else you wish. That makes you a lucky person, and—even better—you'll have created that luck yourself.

29

◆

FOLLOW YOUR OWN PATH

My wife's father was a farmer. It wasn't what he wanted to do, but the farm had been in the family for generations and he was expected to take it over. Because he had no interest in farming, he wasn't a particularly good one and never enjoyed it. Like millions of people, he gave in to pressure from others, his parents in this case. The pressure was well-intentioned but robbed him of the life he could have had. This sort of expectation is less common today than it was, but family expectations and peer pressure still put many people into careers they're not interested in and have no aptitude for. You don't have to do what other people want. Living the life someone else tells you to live is never fulfilling, no matter how lucrative or prestigious it may appear. Imagine waking up one morning when you're eighty years old, full of regrets because you failed to do what you knew you were put on this earth to accomplish.

Bronnie Ware, an Australian palliative care nurse, looked after patients in the final days or weeks of their lives. She wrote a blog post about what they told her, and ultimately wrote a book called *The Top Five Regrets of the Dying*. The biggest regret her patients told her was: "I wish I had the courage to live a life true to myself, not the one others expected of me" (https://bronnieware.com/blog/regrets-of-the-dying/).

It can be hard to leave the path that others encouraged you to take. After all, that's the path that in the past proved to be a tried and tested route to security, status, and a well-paying job. When you start on a path that resonates for you, you'll take on a degree of uncertainty and risk but will lead a life of happiness, passion, and meaning.

You're likely to be fearful at times. My former dentist hated dentistry and wanted to pursue a career in photography. As he worked on his patients' teeth, he told them about his dream of becoming a photographer. Many of them encouraged him to do it, as they had seen his work displayed in his office. Unfortunately, he never did; he was too scared to leave. He was making a good living as a dentist and had a large house, expensive car, and a vacation home. His children were at private schools. The thought of risking his lifestyle prevented him from following his dream, and he died in his middle fifties without ever knowing what he could have accomplished.

Everyone has fears, and you have to overcome them if you want to follow your own path. There'll be problems to resolve, even well along the road, and there'll be times of fear and worry, too. Everyone experiences these, even people who are on the wrong path. Don't let fear hold you back. Recognize it and continue moving forward.

Some people discover the right path at an early age. Jane Goodall, the British primatologist, is an excellent example of someone who followed her own path. It probably started when she was a young child and her father gave her a stuffed chimpanzee toy called Jubilee. This started her interest in animals and she still has the chimpanzee, who sits on her dresser in her London home. When he was twelve years old, a school teacher encouraged my father to take up medicine rather than become a carpenter. Despite strong parental opposition, my father became a surgeon and spent his life following his own path.

Others find their path late. The American folk artist Anna Mary Robertson Moses (1860–1961), better known as Grandma Moses, had always dabbled in art but didn't start to fulfill her childhood dream until she was in her sixties. Eleven years later, in 1938, an art collector named Louis J. Caldor bought about twenty of her paintings, and a year later her work was included in the New York Museum of Modern Art exhibition. By the time she died, she had painted more than fifteen hundred works of art.

It's never too early or too late to start on your path. Find out what's truly important to you, and then pursue it. Only then will you lead the life you're meant to live, and only then will you be truly lucky.

30

◆

Practice the
Golden Rule

The Golden Rule states: treat others the way you would
like to be treated. The concept of the Golden Rule
dates back at least four thousand years and is taught in
most of the world's major religions. The oldest example of
the golden rule is found in *Hitopadehsa*, an ancient book
of fables of India: "One should always treat others as they
wish to be treated." *The Eloquent Peasant* was a popular
story in Egypt during the time of the Middle Kingdom (c.
2040–c. 1650 BCE) that contained the words: "Now this is
the command: Do to the doer to cause that he do thus to
you" (Wilson, 121). About twenty-five hundred years ago,
Confucius wrote: "What you do not want done to yourself,
do not do to others." A contemporary example was said by
the American biochemist and two-time Nobel prizewinner,
Dr. Linus Pauling (1901–1994), in response to a question

he was asked about ethics after a lecture he gave at Monterey Peninsula College, California, in 1961: "I have something that I call my Golden Rule. It goes something like this: 'Do unto others twenty-five percent better than you expect them to do unto you.'…The twenty-five percent is for error" (Helliwell, 145).

The Golden Rule is simple and easy to understand. Many people follow it instinctively: they're caring, kind, and empathetic, and naturally treat other people as well as they can. There are times when the Golden Rule may not apply. The relationships between a parent and child, teacher and student, and employer and employee are good examples. Even so, an employer should treat his employee in the way he would like to be treated if the roles were reversed. As everyone is different, there'll also be times when you need to treat people the way they want to be treated rather than the way you'd want to be treated in the same situation. If you're a salesperson, for instance, you'll be more successful if you find out how each potential customer wants to be treated before investing much time in the process.

The one-word version of the Golden Rule is "empathy." If you're tempted to do something that might hurt someone, ask yourself how you'd feel if someone did the same thing to you. If you wouldn't want it done to you, the other person would probably feel the same, and you shouldn't do it. When you put yourself in the other person's position, you'll be empathizing with them.

Unfortunately, the Golden Rule is not always easy to follow in practice, as everyone has to deal with difficult people from time to time. However, these are the times in which you most need to practice it. You must, for instance, treat others with kindness and gentleness, even if they don't show the same respect to you. When this happens, you'll refrain from returning unpleasantness with more unpleasantness. Hopefully, your love and compassion will soften other people's attitudes and they'll respond to your innate goodness and warmth. However, there are no guarantees.

When you treat others with compassion, kindness, and respect, you'll feel differently about yourself. People will respond and trust you in return. This can open up opportunities you might never have been presented with otherwise. This shows that practicing the Golden Rule can increase your luck. A quotation that has been attributed to both Bridget O'Donnel and Bette Davis says: "Your luck is how you treat people."

31

◆

EVERYONE IS IMPORTANT

R ecently, I attended the funeral of a good friend who died far too young. She was always enthusiastic and keen to give anything a go. She loved people; wherever she went, she asked people their names and remembered them when their paths crossed again. She spent the last two years of her life in the hospital and became everyone's favorite patient, making friends with all the staff and showing interest in them and their lives. She had a large funeral at which the people who stood up to speak told us how she had made them feel recognized and validated. Doctors and hospital cleaning staff alike told us how they'd go and see her whenever they felt stressed or in need of a boost. Her interest in and love for everyone she met was the key factor of her life. While her life wasn't easy, she constantly enriched the lives of others. In her eyes, everyone was important.

The Persian poet Rumi (1207–1273) wrote: "You are not a drop in the ocean. You are the entire ocean in a drop." In other words, you encapsulate the entire ocean in one person. This means that you and everyone else are important. You are part of Divine Intelligence and possess the entire intelligence of the universe. There is a whole ocean of possibilities inside you, which means you can achieve whatever you want. How can you not be important?

If it is true that everyone is important, that means it is also important to treat everyone well, including people who aggravate and annoy you, take advantage of you, or who are rude and unpleasant *just as much* as those who love you, believe in you, teach you important lessons, and bring out the best in you.

As everyone is important, you never know what person will provide you with a lucky opportunity. A homeless person or someone doing a minimum wage job may give you a snippet of wisdom that will change your life. You probably treat authority figures with respect because they might be able to help you directly or introduce you to people who can. However, you should also treat less important people with the same degree of respect—they have knowledge and contacts that you don't. Their knowledge might be more useful to you than that of people who seem more important. You also have to remember that those you might consider less important might hold a much more senior position in the future and will remember how you treated them when you first met.

Let others know how important they are by acknowledging them. At the very least, say hello and thank you. When I was twenty-one and living in Glasgow, Scotland, I thanked the person who looked after the travel arrangements in the publishing company I worked for, as he'd arranged for me to have a few days' work in the London office, which gave me the opportunity to spend time with my girlfriend. A few months later, he gave me two tickets for the Edinburgh Tattoo, which my girlfriend (now wife) and I thoroughly enjoyed. That was a wonderful stroke of luck for both of us. When I thanked him again afterward, I asked him why he'd given them to me when there were hundreds of other people he could have passed them on to. He told me that it was because everyone took him for granted and I was the only person who'd ever gone out of their way to thank him.

Treating everyone as important will enrich your life. It will also provide you with lucky opportunities.

32

◆

MENTORING

Mentors can increase your luck in many ways. They can introduce you to influential people, teach you valuable skills, and provide opportunities to practice them. They'll act as sounding boards for your ideas, and provide help and encouragement. A mentor will have your best interests at heart, and will become a good friend whom you can contact at any time for information and advice.

Some mentors will become lifelong friends, while others will stay with you just long enough to get you started. Many years ago, I had three beehives, and was given valuable help and advice on how to look after them by an elderly man who lived nearby. Once he'd taught me what I needed to know, we went our different ways. Some of my teachers at school were also short-term mentors who saw potentials in me that I hadn't yet recognized. Although the help they gave me was short-term, it has been useful to me ever since. Many years ago, a taxi driver in Johannesburg gave me some valuable ideas in the course of a single cab ride. I'd consider him a short-term mentor, as I was able to make good use of his suggestions.

Mentors have always come into my life when I needed them; I don't recall ever looking for one. However, there's no reason why you shouldn't seek out a mentor if you're ready. Seek out someone who's knowledgeable in the area that interests you and appears to be open and friendly. Ask this person if you can contact them for advice every now and again. Most people will feel flattered and readily agree. Over a period of time, that person will gradually become your mentor. Of course, not everyone will want to become a mentor. If necessary, go through the process as many times as necessary until you find the right person.

A good mentor will be willing to share their skills, expertise, and knowledge with you. The person will be enthusiastic, positive, and honest and will be respected by colleagues and have a good reputation. A mentor will take a personal interest in the relationship and have a strong desire for the mentee to succeed. They will provide guidance, honest feedback, and a shoulder to lean on. The mentor must set a good example in the way they live, which is often the biggest lesson you'll learn.

Once you reach a certain age, people will start asking you if you could mentor them. I think a large percentage of people who have been mentored ultimately become mentors themselves. A good example is Warren Buffett, who was mentored by Benjamin Graham and later became a mentor for many people, including Bill Gates.

John Wooden (1910–2010), the great basketball player and coach, said: "Everything in the world has been passed down. Every piece of knowledge is something that has been shared by someone else. If you understand it as I do, mentoring becomes your true legacy. It is the greatest inheritance you can give to others. It is why you get up every day—to teach and be taught."

There are many satisfactions in mentoring others, including the feelings of pride when someone you've mentored goes on to do well in life. There's a sense of joy in passing on information to people who are ready to receive it. Usually, the person you're mentoring will be younger than you and will give you the attitudes and insights of a different generation. This gives you additional opportunities that you might have missed out on otherwise.

Whenever you help someone else, you benefit the whole world. Even though this help might be tiny in the scheme of things, the universe will ultimately reward you. Fifty years ago, when I was in India, I learned a Hindu saying that said whenever you do a good deed, the universe expands; whenever you do a bad deed, the universe contracts. Mentoring is certainly a good deed, and you will receive good luck as a result.

33

◆

It Is Never Too Late

It's never too late to change your life and increase your luck. There are many examples of people who did amazing things later in life, showing that physical age has nothing to do with how lucky you are.

Age is largely a state of mind. Many years ago, a friend of mine in the UK told me that he felt old, as most people in his industry were under the age of forty. At the grand old age of thirty-eight he was wondering if he could start again in a different field. He enjoyed playing poker, and his friends encouraged him to teach others how to play the game. He started a school to teach people how to play poker. This small, part-time venture is now a thriving full-time business.

A retired man in my city opened up a fruit and vegetable shop when he was sixty-seven. Twenty years later after building up a chain of stores, he stopped working every day but is still one of the company's directors.

A striking example of a late bloomer was Captain James Arruda Henry whose autobiography, *In a Fisherman's Language*, was published in 2011 when he was ninety-eight. Even more remarkable is the fact that he was illiterate until he was ninety-one. As the German mystical poet Rainer Maria Rilke (1875–1926) said: "You are not too old, and it is not too late."

Colonel Harland Sanders (1890–1980) founded Kentucky Fried Chicken at the age of sixty-five, with the help of a social security check for $105.00. By the time he died, there were six thousand KFC franchised restaurants around the world.

These people didn't put a time or age limit on what they wanted to do. They didn't care what other people thought or said. They decided to ignore the opinions of others, follow their own dreams, and do something they considered worthwhile.

A study published in *Science* (November 4, 2016) looked at the careers of nearly three thousand physicists and found that age had no bearing on when they would produce their best work (https://science.sciencemag.org /content/354/6312/aaf5239). Most people become more cautious as they grow older. This attitude can hold them back and make them fearful when they find a lucky opportunity. I'm sure the famous American astronaut John Glenn

(1921–2016) didn't feel that fear when he became the oldest person to fly into space when he was seventy-seven years old. If you're in your senior years, you might have to deliberately put your fears aside and focus on developing your courage and determination to ensure you make the most of the opportunities that come your way.

Maturity can be an advantage in many ways. You'll have years of life experience behind you and will have hopefully developed patience, empathy, and wisdom. If you're concerned about your age, spend time evaluating your skills and interests, and decide which one, or more, you'd like to pursue. There's no rule that says "it's too late." As soon as you start, opportunities will come your way, and your luck will increase.

34

✦

Act As if You Are Lucky

No one is lucky all the time, but some people seem to receive more than their share of good luck. A lot of this is due to a positive, optimistic view of life. These people expect to be lucky and usually are. Lucky people are busy spotting opportunities and acting on them, while unlucky people are complaining about everything wrong with their lives. The law of attraction has a role to play here: lucky people expect good things to happen, and consequently they attract good things to them. It becomes a self-fulfilling prophecy.

A lady I knew many years ago always said, "that's typical of me," whenever anything went wrong. It was a concerning thing to hear, as her life seemed to be a series of mishaps, small and large. I tried to get her to change her words whenever things went wrong to: "That's not like me." Unfortunately, she wasn't willing to try it. I believe her life would have changed if she'd been prepared to do it. If she'd used positive affirmations as well, there's no telling what she might have achieved.

I knew a billionaire when he was a young man starting out in his career. He had a small printing business in the basement of an old building. He didn't want his customers to see where he worked or the age and condition of his machinery, so he called on all his customers personally. He always wore a smart suit, and drove an old Mercedes-Benz. This created an atmosphere of prosperity and success. He acted as if he was successful, and it didn't take long until success was attracted to him.

Lucky people do the same thing. They act as if they're lucky and expect good luck to occur. They have the same ups and downs in life as everyone else, but they remain optimistic, knowing that the bad times will pass and they'll shortly experience some good luck. They choose to look on the bright side of life.

A man I know has an uncanny knack for knowing when to buy and sell businesses. When I asked him how he managed to be so lucky, he told me that he always focused on positive outcomes. He'd visualize the result he wanted in his mind ahead of time. Before buying a business, he'd decide on the maximum amount he'd be willing to pay for it and would then visualize himself negotiating the purchase for a price well below that figure. In his mind's eye he'd see himself waking up in the morning, feeling lucky, and heading to wherever the contract was going to be signed. He'd feel lucky as he walked into the office to conduct the negotiations, exchanged pleasantries, and then sat down to discuss the proposed purchase. Once the details had been agreed upon, he'd see himself signing the contract, shaking hands, and returning home. He'd visualize the sale of the business in exactly the same way. He's had a highly successful career with the help of visualization and by acting as if he were lucky. He told me that if you act as if you're lucky, it will soon become a natural part of your life, and you'll believe you are lucky. Knowing with every fiber of your being that you're lucky, you'll soon start attracting all the luck you'll ever need.

35

❖

Today Is a
Lucky Day

Every day can be a lucky day. In fact, every day can be your lucky day. However, you can't be truly lucky until you believe that you're lucky. Everyone's different, and some people are born knowing that they have the ability to be lucky. Other people have subconscious fears and doubts that undermine their potential for luck. These are obviously false beliefs. After all, if someone else can be lucky, there's no reason why they can't be, too.

All you need do is build up your belief that you are lucky. Norman Vincent Peale (1898–1993) wrote: "Believe in yourself! Have faith in your abilities! Without a humble but reasonable confidence in your own powers you cannot be successful or happy" (Peale, 1). When I was about twenty, I saw Tennessee Williams's play, *A Streetcar Named Desire* for the first time. In the final scene, one of the characters tells another: "You know what luck is? Luck is believing you're lucky" (Williams, 98). Once you believe in yourself and luck, everything else will fall into place.

Here are six ways to increase your self-belief:

1. Constantly affirm to yourself that you're lucky and deserve the very best that life has to offer. You might affirm: "I am a lucky person and today is my lucky day." (See chapter 5, on affirmations.)

2. Constantly visualize yourself as the lucky person you're going to be. (See chapter 21, on visualization.)

3. Constantly see yourself as being equal to everyone else. People with low self-belief often view others as being better than them. In actuality, no one is better or more deserving than you.

4. At least once a week do something that scares you. Get out of your comfort zone and discover how good it feels to do something you've been scared of attempting.

5. Take control of your thoughts. We're all much harder on ourselves than we are on anyone else. Whenever you find yourself thinking a negative thought, remind yourself that you're the person who created it, and you no longer want it. Deliberately turn the thought around, say an affirmation, or think something happy or positive instead. You might, for instance, start

thinking of five things in your life that you're grateful for. Changing your thoughts can change your life.

6. Congratulate yourself for every success you make, no matter how small it may be. Recently, I met a woman who was enjoying a cup of coffee. She told me that the coffee was her reward for remembering to take her medication.

Your luck will change as soon as you start doing this. As an old Japanese proverb says: "The day you decide to do it is your lucky day."

36

◆

Make the
Most of Every
Opportunity

American motivational speaker and author Earl Nightingale (1921–1989) said: "There is more opportunity
hidden in our daily work than most of us could exploit in a
lifetime" (Nightingale, 17). The problem is that most people
seek good luck and opportunities everywhere, except where
they currently are. Opportunities are everywhere. Russell
H. Conwell (1843–1925) was an orator, philanthropist, and
author. His famous book, *Acres of Diamonds*, was originally
a speech that he delivered 6,152 times around the world.
It was first published in book form in 1888 and is still in
print today. It tells the story of a farmer who sold his farm
to search for diamonds. The man who bought the farmer's
property discovered diamonds on the farm and became

incredibly wealthy. The moral is that you can find fortune in your own backyard.

Of course, you might wait forever if you simply sit and expect the right opportunity to fall into your lap. You need to be alert and actively look for potential opportunities. Paul Allen, one of the founders of Microsoft, did this when he saw a magazine cover showing the first microcomputer. It convinced him and Bill Gates that the microcomputer revolution was about to start. They seized the opportunity and changed the world. Thousands of other people must have seen that magazine cover, too, but either didn't recognize the opportunity or were not motivated enough to research the idea further.

Sir Richard Branson, founder of the Virgin media group, has never hesitated to take advantage of opportunity. He said: "Opportunities are like buses, there's always another one coming." This means that you needn't get upset when you miss a potential opportunity, as another one will present itself before long. Obviously, you have to evaluate opportunities you find; not all of them will be suitable for you.

About forty years ago, my brother and I were given the opportunity to buy a lawnmower repair business. The company's figures were good and the owner was prepared to sell it to us at a low price because our father had helped him at one time. It seemed like a wonderful opportunity except for one thing—neither my brother nor myself are good with our hands. If something of mine needs to be repaired, it's usually cheaper for me to employ someone to fix it for me. After discussing it seemingly endlessly, we turned the opportunity down as we didn't possess the right skills to make a success of it.

You need to keep a positive attitude while looking for opportunities. It's amazing how easily negative thoughts manage to creep into our minds. We think things, such as "I can't do that," "It's too hard," "I'll never raise the money," and "I'll have to work twenty hours a day," that often dampen and even kill our enthusiasm. The right opportunity will inevitably take a great deal of time, effort, and money, but it makes no sense to allow negative thoughts to eliminate what might be the perfect opportunity for you. Fear, doubt, and worry—all thoughts created in the mind—are your worst enemies when you're searching for opportunities.

While you're searching for the right opportunity, prepare yourself by learning as much as you can. Be curious and interested in everything you see. Read books, ask questions, take courses, and do anything else you can think of that will broaden your knowledge. You might even find the perfect opportunity while you're doing this. Recently, I read about someone who'd volunteered at a school library, at least partly because it gave him the opportunity to read when he wasn't doing anything else. One of the students was confined to a wheelchair. One day, while he was helping this student, he looked carefully at the wheelchair and was convinced that he could improve the design of it to make it safer and more comfortable. He now owns several patents and runs a business that manufactures wheelchairs.

You should also make a concerted effort to meet as many people as possible. If you remain alert to potential opportunities, you'll be amazed at the number of ideas you'll pick up during casual conversations. You may not have yet met the person who'll give you an opportunity that will give you all the good luck you could ever need.

Once you find the right opportunity, act on it and make it happen. If you don't make the most of the opportunity, someone else will. Here are some suggestions on what to do when you're searching for an interesting opportunity.

1. Spend plenty of time conversing with other people. You'll receive plenty of ideas if you listen carefully.

2. Be curious and ask questions about everything that interests you. If you look at things differently, you'll come up with all sorts of ideas that you might be able to capitalize on.

3. Imagine there are opportunities everywhere, and look at everything you see with new eyes. How could you improve it, and make it more useful or exciting?

4. Does a certain opportunity seem right for you? If, for instance, you're an athletic person who loves spending time outdoors, the opportunity to buy

into a business that researches family histories might not be a good choice. However, it could be the perfect opportunity for someone who is studious and enjoys working indoors.

5. Once you've found an opportunity, evaluate it carefully to decide if you should proceed. There are risks involved with every opportunity, so you need to make sure that the risk is worth taking.

37

◆

Increase Good Karma

Karma is the spiritual law of cause and effect. It's created every moment by our thoughts, words, and actions. If you think good thoughts, speak kindly, and act fairly and honestly, you'll pick up good karma. Conversely, if you think bad thoughts, speak unkindly, and act dishonestly, you'll create bad karma. If you treat everyone badly, sooner or later you might discover that people treat you badly. You ultimately reap what you sow. Karma is the harvest you reap. Although karma is usually associated with Eastern religions, it's also mentioned in the Bible: "Be not deceived; God is not mocked: for whatsoever a man soweth, that shall he also reap" (Galatians 6:7).

Many people do good things because they expect or want something in return. Doing this doesn't create good karma, as their intent isn't pure. You build up good karma only when your thoughts, intentions, and actions are honest and good for everyone involved.

As you're creating karma all the time, it makes good sense to create as much good karma as possible. Good luck or bad luck are the results of your actions in the past. You ultimately get what you deserve, as does everyone else. However, you have no control over when you get to reap your karmic harvest.

A friend of mine frequently says, "What goes around, comes around." Instead of getting angry whenever someone or something annoys him, saying these words keeps him calm and relaxed.

Building up good karma is simply common sense. If you want to lead a happy life, following the Golden Rule and treating people well will pay rich rewards. In addition to this, while good things are happening to you, you'll also receive your share of well-deserved good luck.

There are many ways to build up good karma, such as the following:

1. Be honest. People will be less likely to trust you if they catch you telling a lie. The old saying "honesty is the best policy" is just as true today as it ever was. A good exercise is to see how long you can go without telling a single lie.

2. Help others. Every time you help someone, you help yourself at the same time. It also means that

other people will be more likely to help you when you need it.

3. Be kind. Empathize with others and spread kindness and compassion everywhere you go.

4. Express gratitude. Everyone likes to be appreciated and you can improve the day for many people by simply saying a sincere thank you.

5. Forgive others. Holding grudges is painful and holds you back. Releasing the bad feelings eliminates the negativity and allows you to start gaining good karma again.

6. Do the right thing. When you find yourself tempted to do one thing while knowing that you should do the other, take a minute to think about the possible consequences to yourself, even if no one else will ever know. How important is your reputation to you?

7. Mentor and teach. Mentoring and teaching give you the opportunity to pass on the knowledge you've learned to others. It's deeply satisfying and provides benefits for everyone involved.

8. Compliment others. Giving a genuine compliment is a valuable gift that costs nothing, but has a positive effect on others. If you look for the good in others, you'll find plenty of opportunities to give people sincere compliments.

9. Pray. Pray for the people you love, and pray for all of humanity. Pray for the health of our planet. While you're praying, send your love to all living things.

38

◆

Superstitions and Folklore

Superstition is based entirely on chance, as superstitious practices are intended to either attract good luck or end a run of bad luck. In fact, luck is commonly anthropomorphized as "Lady Luck," an unpredictable and capricious figure who can help us in one moment and turn against us the next. Because of this, she has to be constantly wooed in an attempt to keep her on our side.

Throughout history, people have carried lucky charms and amulets in the hope of attracting good luck or to avert bad luck. Even today, countless millions of dollars are spent each year on good luck charms. Many people carry lucky rabbit's feet, four-leaf clovers, miniature horseshoes, and other charms to help them gain good luck. Even people who claim they aren't superstitious wear lucky charms, because "it can't hurt, and might help." A sales representative

I know carries a St. Christopher medallion everywhere he goes. He told me that it works, even though he doesn't believe in it. For him, the proof is that he's never had an accident. Niels Bohr (1885–1962), the Nobel Prize winning physicist, had a horseshoe hanging over his office door. "Surely you don't believe that will make any difference to your luck?" a colleague once asked. "No," Niels agreed, "but I hear it works even for those who don't believe."

Few people will walk under a ladder or open an umbrella indoors. People still knock on wood to avert fate, and say "God bless you" when someone sneezes.

Even wealthy and well-known people have charms and rituals to ensure continued good luck. John D. Rockefeller Sr. carried a lucky stone everywhere he went. Dr. Samuel Johnson, the eighteenth-century British writer and critic, was extremely superstitious and touched every post he passed when out walking. He avoided all the cracks between paving stones and always stepped out of doors using his right foot. President Franklin D. Roosevelt had a phobia of the number thirteen. He wouldn't do anything important on a day or time that included that number. Harry S. Truman had a horseshoe placed above the door of the Oval Office.

Famous athletes are often highly superstitious, too: Tiger Woods has always worn red shirts and Michael Jordan wore a pair of powder-blue practice shorts from his alma mater, the North Carolina Tar Heels, under his Chicago Bulls ones.

There are many famous sayings that relate to superstition and luck.

"Beginner's luck" describes the initial good luck that people have when they start anything new.

"Lucky at cards, unlucky in love" is an old proverb that means you can have some things, but you can't have everything.

Throughout history, people have conducted superstitious practices to try to gain good luck. Even today, millions of people, myself included, carry good luck charms. (See chapter 44, Lucky Charms.) Obviously, a large percentage of the world's population still believe that they work.

Because life in past centuries was full of dangers, both real and imagined, folk traditions contained a great deal of advice on how to attract good luck. Many of their techniques may seem ridiculous today, but people will try anything to put luck on their side when they feel uncertain about their futures.

People all around the world cross their fingers to attract good luck when starting something new, or are about to take a minor risk. Traditionally, people also crossed their fingers while telling a lie, because they believed this prevented the devil from catching them. Some people cross their fingers while passing graveyards for the same reason.

Knocking on wood, or touching wood if you're from the United Kingdom, dates back to Pagan times when people believed that trees possessed souls that housed gods. Because of this, trees could be asked to protect crops, provide rain during times of drought, help infertile couples become pregnant, and gain good luck. Today, knocking on wood is usually done to provide protection, and to acknowledge the role that luck has played in our success.

It's a sign of good luck if you see a pin and pick it up. This applies only to straight pins and closed safety pins. It's too late to pick up an open safety pin, as all the luck will have vanished. To be lucky, a straight pin also needs to have its point facing away from you. If you pick up a pin that's facing toward you, it is said that you'll pick up sorrow.

It's also considered good luck to pick up a penny, and many people carry them as a lucky charm. Most children know the rhyme: "Find a penny, pick it up. All day long you'll have good luck." This is an ancient superstition that dates back to when metal, especially iron, was believed to avert evil spirits. Another possibility is the belief that finding a penny is considered a gift from the gods, and consequently brought good luck to anyone who found it.

Children are encouraged to make a wish when they blow out the candles on their birthday cake. The wish will be granted if the person blows out all the candles with a single puff. In addition, the person will have good luck until the next birthday. This superstition dates back to the ancient Greeks, who placed candles on top of cakes to try to gain favor from Artemis, the moon goddess. The cake symbolized the moon.

Almost everyone has made a wish while pulling on a wishbone, hoping they will break off the larger piece of the bone. This superstition dates back thousands of years to the ancient Etruscans. They used the movements of chickens to predict the future, and because the wishbone somewhat resembled the human groin, it became a symbol of fertility and ultimately, good luck.

It's also lucky to pick up a button, a coin, a four-leaf clover, a pencil, a postage stamp, a yellow ribbon, or anything purple. To gain the luck, the object needs to be picked up.

An old belief says that wearing anything blue increases your luck. This is because heaven was thought to be up in the blue sky, which meant that the color blue obviously repelled anything negative. Brides still wear something blue to attract good luck.

When you get dressed in the morning, you should put the right sock or stocking on first. You should also put your right arm into a shirt or blouse first. Doing this ensures you'll enjoy good luck during the day. There's specific advice for men on how to put on their trousers. If a man puts his right leg into his trousers first, he'll always be the master of the house. If he puts his left leg in first, he'll receive little respect from other members of the household, and is likely to be henpecked. The man who puts both legs into his trousers at the same time will attract good luck.

Wearing new clothes on New Year's Day provides a year of good luck. Wearing red clothes on this day is highly lucky and is a sign that you'll receive many new items of clothing during the upcoming year.

Superstitions serve a useful purpose as they reduce anxiety, and provide people with confidence and a sense of being in control. All of these feelings can—and often do—affect the outcome. Carrying a lucky charm, or anything else that is believed to create good luck, has been shown to help people perform better than they would have done without it. (Damisch, 2010)

39

◆

Serendipity

The word "serendipity" was coined by the English writer Horace Walpole (1717–1797) on January 28, 1754. It means "making fortuitous and unexpected discoveries by accident." Walpole created the word from the title of an old story called *The Three Princes of Serendip*. This told the story of three princes and their search for a missing camel. Serendip was an early name for modern-day Sri Lanka.

There are many examples of serendipitous discoveries.

A serendipitous discovery changed the course of modern medicine. In 1928, Alexander Fleming (1881–1955), a Scottish medical researcher, returned from a two-week vacation and found a mold growing on his accidentally contaminated staphylococcus culture. He noticed that the mold prevented the staphylococci from growing. This happy accident led to the discovery of penicillin. Fleming described the moment: "One sometimes finds what one is not looking for. When I woke up just after dawn on September 28, 1928, I certainly didn't plan to revolutionize all medicine by discovering the world's first antibiotic, or bacteria killer. But I guess that was exactly what I did" (Jackson, 43). Sir Alexander Fleming was awarded the Nobel Prize in Physiology or Medicine in 1945.

The Post-it Note came into being when Spencer Silver, a 3M scientist, created a weak adhesive. For years, he struggled to find a use for it. Serendipitously, Art Fry, a colleague, sang in a church choir and discovered he could use it to keep bookmarks in place on his hymn book. (https://www.post-it.com/3M/en_US/post-it/contact-us/about-us/)

A wonderful example of serendipity is oshimizu water. In the 1980s, when Japan Railways East constructed a tunnel through Mount Tanigawa, the engineers had constant problems with water seepage. While their designers were designing an expensive drainage system, a maintenance worker sampled the water, and said it was so good it should be bottled and sold as a premium drink rather than simply drained away. After testing the water, Japan Railways East decided to enter the premium bottled water business and called their drink *oshimizu*. Before long, oshimizu water vending machines were on the platforms of every station. The water is created from the pure snow on Mount Tanigawa's snow and accumulates minerals as it slowly seeps through the rock.

Serendipity is always good as it's a lucky accident. Luck is capricious and can be good or bad. As serendipity occurs accidentally, it might seem that it can't be encouraged to occur. In fact, it can. You can activate serendipity with your curiosity, initiative, attitude, enthusiasm, optimism, and actions. Sometimes, it might be as simple as perseverance.

The key is to be curious and flexible. One of the definitions of serendipity is to accidentally find something while looking for something else. While you're searching for whatever it might be, you're naturally focused and alert. Accompanied with flexibility, this mindset can provide you with an abundance of good luck.

Seizing opportunities is a good way to encourage serendipity. Sometimes it's easy to turn down invitations to events that you think might be boring, or you won't know many people who'll be attending. However, if you accept and make the effort to go, you'll meet new people, and be exposed to their thoughts and ideas. You might even meet someone who'll offer you an opportunity you'd have missed if you'd turned down the invitation. It can be scary to go to events on your own, but you'll be exposed to more opportunities if you do.

Talking to strangers is another way to open yourself up to serendipity. A writer friend of mine met his agent on a shuttle bus at a book convention. It turned out to be fortuitous for both of them. Many years ago, when I was on the

Kowloon to Hong Kong ferry, I accidentally overheard part of a conversation two young women were having. I asked them a question about what they were talking about, and they kindly gave me a detailed reply. That serendipitous encounter gave me the idea for my book *Spirit and Dream Animals*, which was published a few years later, and received the COVR Award for the best divination book of 2012. It was definitely a lucky day for me. If I'd held back and not taken advantage of what I'd heard, that book would never have been written, and I wouldn't be an award-winning author today.

Asking questions encourages serendipity, too. Most people enjoy sharing their knowledge with others. This often leads to interesting conversations, and may alert you to serendipitous opportunities.

You can encourage serendipity into your life in many ways. You could do something that takes you out of your normal, everyday routine. You might visit a museum, attend a show, take a class, or watch a sport that you've never followed before. You could read a magazine that you wouldn't normally buy, walk through a park you haven't visited before, and chat with people in elevators. It doesn't matter what it is, as long as it's something you don't normally do. Even changing how you get to work can provide you with new ideas. Turn off your mobile devices, smile readily, be approachable, and talk with as many people as you can while you're going about your normal, everyday life. Seren-dipitous experiences can provide you with lucky opportuni-ties and occur frequently when you get out of your comfort zone and explore something new or different.

40

◆

FAILURE

N o one likes to fail, but failure can sometimes be good. Throughout history, numerous people have lost battles, but have ultimately won the war. When Swiss biophysicist Jacques Dubochet won the Nobel Prize for chemistry in 2017, he said: "It was serendipity, luck, and some major failures that led me to the key aha moment" (www.embl.fr /aboutus/alumni/news/news_2017/20171116_Dubochet -Serendipity/).

Thomas Edison was one of the most famous inventors and innovators the world has ever seen. Along with his many successes, he also experienced his share of failures— but he didn't call them failures. He famously said: "I have not failed 10,000 times—I've just found 10,000 ways that will not work" (Bloom, xiv).

Many successful people have experienced failure but they had more than enough courage to continue. They take personal responsibility for the situation they're in. Failure taught them much-needed lessons and enabled them to start again with a new understanding about what they needed to do to succeed. Failure isn't fatal unless it kills all your dreams and you fail to get up again. Henry Ford said: "failure is simply the opportunity to begin again, this time more intelligently" (Ford, 19–20).

There are many reasons why people fail. They may have overreached themselves, made poor decisions, stopped working hard, or failed to keep a close eye on their resources. The industry they were in might have changed dramatically. The product they manufactured and sold might have been superseded. None of these things matter in the grand scheme of things, as long as the people involved get through the period of pain and anguish, recognize their role in what happened, learn from the experience, and start again. Because of what they will have learned from the experience, they'll be more shrewd and better prepared to achieve their goals in the future. Failure might sound like bad luck but sometimes it can be good luck, as it forces you to take stock, hopefully learn from the experience, and start again.

Even if it turns out to be good luck in the long term, it can still be devastating when it happens. Fortunately, there is a process to help you move forward again after failure.

1. Failing feels bad, and your emotions will be in a state of turmoil. Allow yourself time to feel bad, but don't let the feelings break you. Accept the situ-

ation, and gradually start doing things that nurture you. You might like to spend time with friends, go for long walks, watch movies, or do anything else that helps you as your emotions subside.

2. Accept responsibility for your part in the failure. Remind yourself that everyone makes mistakes. This failure doesn't define you. You can learn from the experience and start again. Almost every big success has come after failures and setbacks. You are not a failure unless you give up.

3. Analyze the experience from a dispassionate point of view. What actually went wrong? Was the failure out of your control? What, if anything, could you have done to prevent the failure from occurring? What have you learned from the experience? What will you do differently next time?

4. Realize that constantly dwelling on your failure will not change anything. All it does is keep you chained to the past.

5. Discuss what happened with someone you trust. Doing this will help you sort out your feelings, and will help you come to terms with what happened. Discussing the situation with a friend will help you see the situation through someone else's eyes.

6. Start moving forward again. The fact that you failed last time doesn't mean you'll fail this time. Failure is a temporary situation. Look at the failure as a learning lesson that will help you succeed in the future. Make plans and start something new.

Everyone experiences disappointments, setbacks, and failures. Some people might consider it the result of bad luck. However, people who analyze what went wrong, take their share of the blame, and start moving forward again will learn from the experience and experience good luck in the future.

41

◆

DRISHTI

Drishti is a Sanskrit word that means "sight." It relates to using the eyes to focus attention on something specific for a particular purpose. In yoga, it's used to focus on one of nine different points while the person meditates or practices different asanas. It creates self-awareness, and increases the effectiveness of the meditation. Yogis use drishti to enable their eyes to perceive an inner reality that isn't normally visible. It enables them to see the divine in everything. Drishti can help you make friends, develop concentration, and focus on what you want.

You can practice drishti by using your eyes to send encouraging, empathetic, kindhearted, compassionate energy to everyone you encounter as you go about your everyday life. The muscles around your eyes should be relaxed, and your gaze needs to be soft. It's unlikely that anyone will know you're practicing drishti, but they will notice the effects of your love, kindness, and positive energy, and are likely to respond by sending similar energy back to you. You'll communicate well with others and find it easier to express your ideas. You'll also meet more people and make more friends. All of these provide opportunities for good luck.

Drishti is used in yoga to develop focus and concentration. It's hard to concentrate on any activity, including yoga, if the eyes freely wander from one distraction to another. Your attention is quite naturally directed at whatever you happen to be looking at. Consequently, practitioners of Ashtanga Vinyasa and other schools of yoga focus on different places depending on which asana they are performing. This single-pointed focus helps to still the mind.

Drishti also means inner vision, intelligence, and wisdom. Many people meditate by sitting with their eyes closed and directing their inner gaze upward to the area of their third eye in the center of the forehead. Though the eyes are closed, the gaze is focused on a single spot, enabling them to concentrate on the meditation. As well as doing this for meditation, you can use it to open yourself up to potentially useful ideas that you'll be able to evaluate and work on.

Once you're relaxed and are focusing on the area of your third eye, ask yourself what you'll be doing in five years' time. Wait and see what thoughts come into your mind. Don't evaluate them. Simply wait patiently and allow whatever ideas and images occur to come into your mind.

Once you've opened your eyes, write down everything that came to you during the meditation. Read it over and make any additions or amendments that occur to you. Place these ideas aside for about twenty-four hours. When you read them again a day later, you'll find your mind will probably have more information to offer you. Write this down, too.

You may find that you're happy with what you recorded. It's more likely that you'll be pleased with some of this five-year forecast, but not so happy with other aspects of it. Think about the future you want to have, and write down the changes you'll need to make to ensure you'll be happy with your way of life five years from now.

At this stage, you'll need to perform another meditation. Relax, focus on your third eye, and visualize the wonderful life you'll be living in five years' time. Become aware of any feelings or sensations you have in your body while doing this. Ask yourself if you're prepared to do whatever is necessary to attain this goal. If the answer's negative, or you feel unpleasant sensations in your body, you need to ask further questions to find out what's holding you back from the future you desire. If the answer's positive, again ask yourself what your life will be like in five years' time. Enjoy knowing that this will become your reality.

When you feel ready, open your eyes and record everything that occurred during the meditation. During the next few weeks, you'll need to create a plan of action to ensure that you stay on target and achieve your goal. Drishti can bring you enormous luck by showing you what you need to do to achieve any goal you set for yourself.

Drishti can also provide you with good luck in another way. You can use the drishti meditation to become closer to the Divine. You may call this God, the Universal Life Force, Divine Spirit, or any other name you wish.

Relax, close your eyes, focus on your third eye, and imagine you're getting closer and closer to God. Imagine yourself in the presence of the Almighty, and experience the incredible power of divine love. Allow this love to enter every cell of your body until every part of you is full of universal love. When you open your eyes, you might feel spaced out for a few minutes. Stand up, walk barefoot on earth or grass, and eat or drink something to become fully grounded again. Afterward, you'll feel centered, balanced, and full of love and compassion.

42

◆

Hunches and
Intuition

Have you ever met someone and instantly felt the person could not be trusted and then later discovered your feeling was correct? Where did that feeling of yours come from? I'm sure you've had instances where you did something even though a small inner voice warned you not to, then later on you regretted not listening to it. It seems we all have a built-in protection system that guides us and keeps on doing so even when we constantly ignore it. Everyone experiences these feelings every now and then. They're called hunches or intuitions. A hunch is a premonition or feeling you get about someone or something. You can't explain it logically, but something inside you tells you that the hunch is true, even though there's no evidence to confirm it. A friend told me that intuition is knowing without knowing.

Some years ago, I gave a talk at a maximum-security prison. I don't remember much about what I said, but vividly remember the question and answer session afterward. In my talk I mentioned the few seconds that can make all the difference. If we pause for a few seconds and listen to our inner voice, we're more likely to make the right decision. One of the inmates stood up at the end and said how he wished he'd paused for a few seconds and listened to his inner voice. If he had, he said, he would not be in jail. Once he said that, several of the other prisoners said the same thing. Some of them had experienced the quiet, little voice but had done what they did anyway. In effect, not listening to their intuition had cost them their freedom.

These examples show how useful our hunches and feeling can be. Fortunately, it's a skill that anyone can develop no matter how logical they think they are.

Relaxation

Hunches and intuition occur more readily when you're quiet and relaxed. Meditation, mindfulness, and yoga are all good ways to find the inner silence within. You might think that your days are too hectic and that you can't set aside time to go into a trance. In actuality, you're doing it all the time. Every time you go into a daydream, for instance, you're effectively in another world for a brief period. While you're in a daydream you can access your inner mind, your intuitive self.

Setting aside a few minutes a day for quiet contemplation helps you in many ways. For one, it reduces stress levels and gives you a few moments of peace, which makes you calmer and more effective during the rest of the day. While you're sitting or relaxing quietly, be aware that your subconscious mind contains the answers to everything that you require. Think about your problem in a quiet, almost dreamy way and ask your subconscious mind to find the answer for you. Once you've done this, allow yourself to feel totally confident that the answer will come.

Our minds are like magnets. Focus on whatever it is you want and your mind will attract it to you. Obviously, you can't expect great insights to come to you every time you sit down quietly by yourself. However, you can create the right conditions to allow it to happen and can spend the time thinking about what it is you want to do.

Remain relaxed and confident that your intuition will provide the answer. Once your relaxation session is over and you get on with your day, your mind will continue to work on the problem and will soon provide you with the answer. This could happen at any time.

Everyone's experienced the situation where they woke up in the morning with the answer to something that seemed hopeless the night before. I find the answer often comes when I'm relaxed and not thinking about the problem. I might be driving in my car, having a shower, enjoying a walk, or watching a comedy on TV. These are all times when my mind has time to mull things over, and I've learned to be receptive no matter when the answer appears.

I know from previous experience that my intuition will provide me with the correct answer, so I usually wait for it with a sense of positive expectancy. I'm also prepared to listen to my inner voice whenever it wants to provide me with information.

Many people I've discussed this with are skeptical about the process. This blocks off their intuition. You need to put any skepticism to one side, and remain positive and aware. Suspending your disbelief is not quite enough.

As your inner mind knows how you really feel, you can't fool it by pretending. If you're skeptical, think back to instances in your life that seem to have no logical explanation. It might have been an extraordinary coincidence. It could have been when you knew exactly what someone was thinking. You may have had a sudden impression about someone which later proved to be correct. It doesn't matter what it was, or how trivial it may have been. Sit down quietly, close your eyes, and relive the incident. Once you've done that, think about your current problem, and ask your intuition to help you find a solution. Be patient. Remain calm and relaxed. Think about your problem in general terms and then carry on with your day. Don't give your concern any more thought. It's usually when you least expect it that the answer will come.

Physical Response

Another method of accessing your intuition is to pay attention to how your body responds. Find a quiet place to sit and relax. When you feel pleasantly relaxed, think about whatever you're considering doing and then focus on your body's response. If, for instance, you're thinking of moving to a different part of the country, you might feel a sense of excitement throughout your body. In this instance, your body is telling you to make the move. Conversely, you might feel tension in your shoulders and neck, or in the pit of your stomach. This is a sign that you should reevaluate the idea and stay living where you are at least until your body starts expressing excitement about the idea.

Be curious in your everyday life, too, and be alert for any sudden insights or hunches that appear unexpectedly in your mind. Your intuition is a perfectly normal and natural mental faculty that you can utilize in every area of your life. It can help you solve problems, make the right decisions, come up with creative ideas, and forecast the future. It can ensure that you're in the right place at the right time. If you use your intuition to do all of this, just imagine how many lucky opportunities you'll receive.

43

◆

The Pendulum

The pendulum is a deceptively simple device that is used to discover hidden information. It can find a stream of water under the ground; locate an item, such as car keys, that has been mislaid; or retrieve information from someone's mind. It can also be used to answer questions, to make decisions, and to implant positive suggestions into someone's subconscious mind. It can also increase your luck.

The pendulum consists of a small weight attached to a thread or chain. Many people use a wedding ring for the weight. Other small weights, such as a key, fishing sinker, small ornament, or jewelry, work just as well. The perfect weight is about three ounces and the best pendulums are roundish in shape, and preferably have a point at the bottom. Commercially made pendulums can be purchased online and at New Age/metaphysical stores.

Most people hold the pendulum with the same hand that they use to write. However, a few people prefer using their other hand; you might like to experiment with that if you have difficulty in getting your pendulum to move. To experiment with a pendulum, sit down and rest your elbow on a table. Hold the thread or chain of your pendulum between your thumb and finger using as little pressure as possible. Your elbow should be the only part of your body touching the table. The palm of your hand should face down and the pendulum should hang about a foot in front of you. Make sure that your arms and legs are uncrossed, as this affects the movements of the pendulum. Swing the pendulum gently back and forth to familiarize yourself with its movement. Allow it to swing in different directions, and then swing it in gentle circles, both clockwise and counterclockwise. While doing this, hold the thread at different lengths to see if the pendulum moves more readily at a particular length. Most people find four to five inches works best for them.

Allow yourself to become used to the movements of the pendulum, and then stop it with your free hand. When the pendulum is still, ask it which movement indicates a positive, or "yes" response. You can ask this question silently or out loud. The pendulum may respond immediately and provide the answer. If you haven't used a pendulum before, it will likely take time before it moves. Everyone is different, but I've yet to meet anyone who can't use a pendulum. It doesn't matter if it takes five minutes, an hour, or a week to move. After you've done it once, you'll be able to do it again, and it won't be long until the pendulum starts moving the instant you ask a question.

Be patient and quietly repeat your question every now and again. It will probably move only slightly at first, but if you keep thinking "yes," it will start moving more and more strongly. Once you've found out which response indicates yes, you can ask your pendulum to indicate other responses such as: no, I don't know, and I don't want to answer. This gives you four possible replies to any question you ask.

Now it's time to practice. Start by asking the pendulum questions that you already know the answers to. You might ask: "Am I female?" If you are, the pendulum will give a positive response. If you're not, it will answer no. You can ask similar questions about your age, marital status, number of children, and so on.

After the pendulum has answered these correctly, you can start asking it questions for which you would like answers. The pendulum can answer these because it can access your subconscious mind and gain information that you're not consciously aware of. There's one caveat. You can override the movements of the pendulum with your will. If, for instance, you're asking about the sex of an unborn child and hope it will be a girl, that is the answer your pendulum will give. If the baby turns out to be a boy, you'll be disappointed. The pendulum said "girl" because you were emotionally involved in the outcome.

You should never use your pendulum as a toy or ask it silly or superficial questions. It will always answer serious questions, but if you use it as a plaything, you'll receive the answers you deserve.

After you've practiced sufficiently, you'll be able to use the pendulum to increase your luck. You can ask your pendulum questions about the character of people you're dealing with, the outcomes of activities you're planning to do, whether you should buy or sell something, and a wide variety of other questions.

You can also use your pendulum to remove negativity and instill a positive and lucky mindset into your subconscious mind. This is a positive ritual to help you lead a happy, worthwhile, and lucky life. I do this every morning. The first step is to remove any negativity in and around you. You do this by deliberately swirling your pendulum in a counterclockwise direction. While the pendulum is moving, say the following words to yourself:

> *I ask the universe to release any negativity that is adversely affecting me in any way. Please release any negativity from any of the environments I'll be in today. Please also release any negativity that might be in the minds and hearts of all the people I love. Please allow any negativity I encounter today to totally dissolve and lose any power to hurt me, or*

anyone else, today. Please replace all the negativity
I encounter with peace, harmony, and love.

I've written these words on an 8 ½ x 11 sheet of cardboard and revolve the pendulum over it as I say them. Usually, I finish saying the words before the pendulum stops moving. When that happens, I repeat the last four words—peace, harmony, and love—over and over until the pendulum stops moving.

I then turn the cardboard over, as I have the positive words written on the other side. This time I swirl the pendulum clockwise and say:

I ask the universe for peace of mind, happiness, joy,
and love in everything I do today. Help me spread
joy and happiness everywhere I go, so that everyone
I encounter will feel better, as a result of my pres-
ence. Please help me be courteous, patient, kind, and
understanding, even in difficult situations. Please
help me make a positive difference to everyone I
encounter today. Please help me recognize any ben-
eficial opportunities that will enable me to progress
in life. Please help me become a magnet for all that
is good, and enable me to attract good luck, and to
see the good in everyone I encounter today.

If necessary, I repeat the final sentence as many times as necessary until the pendulum stops moving. In a sense, this ritual is a powerful affirmation that eliminates negativity and enhances positivity. It enables me to start the day feeling free from stress, worry, or any other form of negativity. At the same time, I'm feeling positive, happy, and lucky. I rarely have a bad day, and I'm sure you'll rarely have one too, once you start doing this morning ritual.

I wear a greenstone amulet attached to a length of cord around my neck virtually everywhere I go. I do this for a number of reasons. First, it was made for me by a friend who lives on the other side of the world, and it reminds me of him. Second, it means I always have a pendulum with me and can ask it questions whenever I wish. Third, I can also attract positivity and good luck to me by swirling it in a clockwise direction. Finally, it is my lucky charm.

44

◆

Lucky Charms

Throughout history, people have worn or carried charms with the hope of attracting good luck and good fortune. Originally, charms were spoken or sung; the word "charm" itself comes from the French word *charme*, which means "song." The blessing given by a priest at the end of a service is a good example of a traditional charm. Over time, people realized that a spoken or sung charm was ephemeral, while something solid was more permanent. Consequently, small objects (especially items that had enjoyed contact with something special) became known as charms. The term "touch wood" relates to this. People felt lucky and blessed when they touched a splinter of wood that they believed came from the cross of Jesus.

People who wear lucky charms expect to receive good luck and are reminded of it every time they see or feel their charm. Scientists have shown that lucky charms work because the people who wear or carry them believe they're protected and will perform better. Such objects also diminish any fear of failure. When you're not afraid to fail, you're willing to take more calculated risks, thereby increasing your chances of success. In other words, believing a charm will bring you luck leads precisely to this outcome. One person I knew described lucky charms as security blankets because they make people feel safe and protected. This might explain why an estimated 24 percent of Americans carry a lucky charm with them at least occasionally (today .yougov.com/topics/lifestyle/articles-reports/2018/07/11 /nearly-quarter-americans-carry-lucky-charm).

Psychologist Lysann Damisch of the University of Cologne, Germany, conducted a series of experiments to test the hypothesis that lucky charms and rituals work. In one experiment, volunteers were asked to putt golf balls into a hole from about four feet away. She told half of them that the ball they were using was a "lucky" ball. The other half used a normal, regular golf ball. In another experiment, the volunteers participated in a handheld dexterity game. Half of them were told: "I'm keeping my fingers crossed for you," while the others were simply told to complete the task. In both of these tests, the volunteers who were exposed to "superstitious thinking" performed significantly better as they "felt lucky." Dr. Damisch conducted further tests involving memory and anagrams, and again the "lucky" volunteers all did better than the other volunteers. She came to the conclusion that the people who wore lucky charms or were told they were lucky felt more confident about their abilities. This caused them to set higher expectations and persist for longer when necessary to achieve the desired result. Although there's nothing magical about it, these superstitious practices make people feel protected, and give them confidence that they can succeed (Damisch, 2010). Another possibility is that people's belief in the power of their charms alters their attitudes, outlook, and confidence and make them "lucky."

A 2003 university study in the United Kingdom demonstrated that people who carry lucky charms not only feel luckier, but actually become luckier as a result (psycnet .apa.org/record/2004-21070-001). No matter what the reason may be, it appears that lucky charms and other superstitions can increase your luck.

Almost anything can be used as a lucky charm, and the best charms are objects that relate to you in some way. It might be something that someone gave you, for instance. I have an acorn on my desk that was given to me almost twenty years ago by my granddaughter. A friend of mine has a lucky bookmark that was given to him when he was about ten years old by a woman who saw him leaving his local library with an armful of books.

The most popular lucky charms today are the four-leaf clover, rabbit's foot, horseshoe, a lucky coin, and the St. Christopher medal.

Four-Leaf Clover

The four-leaf clover is an ancient Irish charm that has been traditionally used to attract good luck. Most people have looked for one at some time in their lives. It's said to be especially lucky if you pick one in May. An old legend says that Eve carried one with her when she was banished from the Garden of Eden. As well as providing luck, the four-leaf clover is also said to eliminate unpleasant surprises. According to folklore, if a young lady finds a four-leaf clover and places it in her right shoe, the next single man she meets will become her husband.

Each leaf represents a different aspect of life that is covered in an old rhyme:

> One leaf is for fame,
>
> And one leaf is for wealth,
>
> And one is for a faithful lover,
>
> And one to bring you glorious health,
>
> Are all in the four-leaved clover.

It's been estimated that there's only one four-leaf clover to every five thousand three-leaf clovers, which explains why they're so hard to find.

Rabbit's Foot

The ancient Celts were the first people to associate rabbits with luck. As rabbits lived underground, people assumed they were familiar with the spirits living in the underworld. Rabbits also reproduce quickly, a trait that was naturally associated with abundance and prosperity.

Over time, the rabbit's foot became associated with fruitfulness and good luck. As rabbits are born with their eyes open, people thought this must give them power over the evil eye. Thousands of years ago, people noticed that the hind legs of a rabbit touch the ground before the front legs. They also dig their burrows using their back legs and warn other rabbits of potential danger by thumping a hind leg. These observations may have led people to believe that a rabbit's luck was stored in its back feet.

A rabbit's foot charm must be kept in the left pocket. Traditionally, the best rabbit's foot charm to have is one that contains the left foot of a rabbit that has been killed at full moon by a cross-eyed person.

Horseshoe

Horseshoes can be purchased, but it's considered better—and luckier—to find one. Traditionally, the horseshoe was hung above the front door to ensure that good luck stayed inside the house, although there are two schools of thought as to whether the horseshoe should be hung with the points facing upward or downward. If the horseshoe points upward, the luck is believed to be caught in the bowl-like shape. This shape is also thought to trap the devil, preventing him from entering the house. If the horseshoe is hung downward, it's said to become a magnet that attracts good luck. The horseshoe's crescent shape is considered protective, and horseshoes are also believed to deter witches and the devil. This is probably because horseshoes are put in place with seven nails, a number that has long been considered spiritual.

Horseshoes are associated with good luck due to metal being considered a gift from the gods in ancient times. Blacksmiths were also considered lucky because they worked with fire and were able to turn the divine material into different shapes. The combination of iron, fire, and blacksmith made for an extremely powerful combination.

If the horseshoe has nails in it when you obtain it, use them when you hang it. Each nail represents a full year of good luck. You need to attach the horseshoe with an odd number of nails to achieve the maximum amount of good luck.

It's important to pick up any horseshoe you find, as it will bring you good luck. If you don't want it, you need to spit on it while making a wish. Once you've done that, toss it over your left shoulder and don't look back to see where it landed.

Small, miniature horseshoes can be bought at jewelry stores. They're usually purchased to add to a charm bracelet but can also be carried with you to attract good luck.

Coin

Lucky coins were originally pennies. This is why we have rhymes such as: "See a penny, pick it up. All day long you'll have good luck." Nowadays, many countries no longer keep pennies in circulation, and the luck has been extended to include coins of any denomination.

A lucky coin is any coin that you happen to find, and the luckiest coin to find is one that was minted in the year of your birth. The luck of a coin is doubled if it's found heads-up. You can keep the coin in your pocket or purse, or possibly turn it into a pendant. Some people keep their lucky coin in one of their shoes. It will attract good luck, no matter how you carry it. A coin that was minted in a leap year is twice as lucky as a regular coin, but instead of carrying it, you should keep it in your kitchen where it will provide unexpected good luck. You need to take care of your lucky coin, as it's believed your luck will take a turn for the worse if you happen to lose it.

About ten years ago, I was walking along a street in Shrewsbury, England, with two friends and noticed a ten pence coin lying in the gutter. I bent down to pick it up, and when I stood up again, one of my friends handed me another coin and said, "Double your luck!" He told me that your luck is doubled if someone immediately hands you a coin of the same denomination as the one you picked up.

Lucky charms can often find you. I still have the two ten pence coins, and whenever I see them, they remind me of both my walk in Shrewsbury, and also how lucky I am. Lucky charms should have some sort of attachment to you. If someone had given me the two coins and told me they were lucky, I probably would have kept them, but they would never have had the same association with luck as the one I found, and the one I was immediately given.

St. Christopher Medal

St. Christopher is revered in the Catholic Church, because it's believed that he carried Christ across a dangerous river. On one occasion, a small child asked to be carried across the river. Christopher was a strong man, but the child appeared to get heavier and heavier the further into the fast-moving current they went. When they eventually reached the other side, the child told him that he was actually Christ and that Christopher had carried the whole world and its creator on his shoulders. Because of this legend, St. Christopher became the patron saint of travelers, and his medal is arguably the most popular good luck charm of all.

Colors

The right color can increase your luck. Everyone has color preferences, and even small children ask their friends what their favorite colors are. While a person's favorite color occasionally changes, most people's favorite color is still the one they chose when they were very young. Consequently, a lucky charm can be anything that includes your lucky color in it. One of my nieces has a cute white fluffy mouse toy that she carries as a lucky charm. Her favorite color is yellow, and she tied a small yellow bow around the mouse's neck to make it more powerful.

You can also use color to help you in different areas of life. You might deliberately wear a red shirt or a red scarf if you were wanting to feel confident. If you wanted to have fun, a bit of yellow would help create the right atmosphere. If you don't happen to have a lucky charm, or an item of clothing, of the color you desire, you can visualize yourself surrounded by that particular color, and then breathe it in with every breath. This is called "color bathing."

Red: Red is a popular color, and is especially favored by extroverts as it relates to enthusiasm, ambition, and power. However, many introverts use it too, as it can help them become more outgoing. Red can help you become optimistic, positive, generous, loving, and forgiving. It can also help you develop leadership qualities and achieve your goals.

Orange: Orange is a warm and friendly color. It will help you get on well with others and make you efficient, well organized, and good at completing tasks you've set for yourself.

Yellow: Yellow is the color of communication and sociability. It can help you express yourself well, entertain others, and develop good ideas. If this is your favorite color, you'll thrive on new and different experiences.

Green: If green is your favorite color, you'll be even-tempered, compassionate, tolerant, and easy to get along with. You'll have a good mind and be good with details. Green is a humanitarian color; many people who like it find satisfaction in a career that involves helping others.

Blue: Blue is the most popular color choice of introverts. However, it can also be a good choice for extroverts as it will give them the tranquility and peace of mind that they lack. If blue is your favorite color, you'll have a creative mind and a good imagination. You dislike being hemmed in or restricted in any way. You thrive on freedom and always need something exciting to look forward to.

Indigo: If you are reserved, sensitive, emotional, and intuitive, indigo is likely to be your favorite color. You are gentle, supportive, and easily hurt. You fall in love easily and are happiest in the company of your family and close friends.

Violet: Violet is the favorite color of people who are sophisticated, discriminating, spiritual, and intuitive. You are likely to be introspective and need quite a bit of time on your own. You might be slightly unusual, as you have a unique point of view and always prefer to do things in your own way.

Silver: Silver is the favorite color of people who are honest, idealistic, caring, and intuitive. They have good self-esteem and enjoy helping others. They are modest and self-effacing.

Gold: Gold is often the favorite color of people who are ambitious and want the very best that life can offer. They are creative thinkers with a great deal of ambitions and energy.

Brown: Brown is the favorite color of people who are down-to-earth, practical, stable, and hardworking. They have the ability to assess a situation at a glance, which enables them to find solutions to problems that other people have been unable to resolve. They are deep thinkers but keep many of their thoughts to themselves.

Black: Many people whose favorite color is black are independent thinkers who have strong views on most topics. They are tenacious, disciplined, and goal-oriented. They can also be highly secretive.

White: White is the favorite color of gentle, quiet, nurturing people. They dislike loud, noisy events and prefer to spend their time with a few close friends. They enjoy time on their own.

You may already have a lucky charm and not know it. It could be an heirloom, something someone gave you at some time, a stone you picked up from a beach, or even a small trinket you've owned since you were a young child. Something from childhood or a memorable event is likely to be meaningful to you and could thus be used to help attract good luck.

45

◆

LUCK IN NATURE

Early people found the world a fearful place and observed nature and the seasons for signs of good and bad luck. Some plants were considered luckier than others. Narcissuses, orchids, peach blossom, hydrangeas, magnolias, peonies, and water lilies are all considered lucky. Yellow flowers, such as chrysanthemums, marigolds, St. John's wort, heliotrope, and sunflowers, were believed to attract love and good luck, especially if they were picked on Midsummer's Eve. Red flowers, such as azaleas, were believed to stimulate virility and passion. Blue flowers increased luck in matters of the heart. Pink and red roses are supposedly the luckiest flowers for love and romance. You can attract good luck by cutting white flowers, such as lilies and Solomon's seal, on the day of the new moon and displaying them in a window where the moon's rays will shine on them.

There are lucky flowers for people born in every month of the year:

- January: Carnation

- February: Violet

- March: Daffodil

- April: Daisy

- May: Lily of the Valley

- June: Honeysuckle

- July: Water Lily

- August: Gladiolus

- September: Morning Glory

- October: Calendula

- November: Chrysanthemum

- December: Narcissus

Holly has been considered a lucky plant since Roman times, when it was custom to give it to friends in midwinter as a gesture of friendship and goodwill. Gradually, the plant became associated with love and marriage, and single people would wear it as a charm to help them attract the right partner. Married people can also wear a holly charm as it ensures the relationship will be successful. In northern Europe, it was hung on doors to create good luck.

This was because they believed wood spirits sheltered from the cold winds inside holly plants, and would protect the home. Holly became associated with Christianity as people believed the crown of thorns that Jesus wore was made of holly. Today, holly is a symbol of Christmas and attracts good luck and happiness to everyone living in the home.

Farmers planted poppies to ensure their crops would grow well. They also provide good luck and help people forget their worries. If you give anyone a bunch of poppies, it must contain thirteen stems—it's considered bad luck to give any other number of poppies in the bouquet.

Daisies and dandelions are traditional symbols of love and romance. Most people have plucked off the petals of a daisy one at a time while chanting, "S/he love me, s/he loves me not." The cottony top of the dandelion can be gradually blown off while reciting each phrase with another puff of air. If the entire top comes off with a single puff, you can make a wish. Charms in the shape of daisies or dandelions provide good luck; if you're single, they'll help you attract a suitable partner.

Sage is an especially lucky plant. According to folklore, it can improve the memory, provide wisdom, avert the evil eye, decrease the pain of childbirth, absorb negativity, and provide good luck. You can also write a wish on a sage leaf and then burn it to send the wish out into the universe. As long as you believe it will work, your wish will be granted. It seems as if everyone should have a sage plant, but this isn't the case. It's considered unlucky to grow sage in your own garden, so it is best acquired from someone else.

A number of flowers were considered unlucky if brought into the home. Arum lilies, blackthorn, and hawthorn were all associated with bad luck and death. Bluebells, ivy, and lilacs were simply unlucky. Dandelions were unlucky and said to cause people to wet their beds. Belladonna, or deadly nightshade, is not only poisonous but also extremely unlucky.

Not many people grow their own peas nowadays, and they miss out on an interesting way to gain good luck. If you're shelling peas and find just one pea in a pod, you'll be lucky for a whole month. If you find nine peas in a single pod, you'll be lucky for a year. Your luck will be doubled if you find one or nine peas in the first pod you shell.

Trees were often planted as an offering of thanks after receiving good luck. Even today, it's common for politicians to plant trees to mark special events. Giving a gift to nature always enhances good luck, and the luck increases as the tree grows and thrives.

You're said to enjoy a year of good luck if you dance around a tree on New Year's Day. However, dancing around your own indoor Christmas tree doesn't work—the tree must be outdoors!

It's considered lucky to catch a leaf as it falls off a tree. Each leaf caught will give you a month of good luck. It's also a sign of good luck if dead leaves blow into your home. However, it's bad luck to carry leaves inside, even accidentally.

It's good luck to hug a tree. You can hug any tree you wish, but it's best to choose a tree that appeals to you aesthetically. There's no right or wrong way to do it. You might wrap your arms around the trunk, and place your cheek against the trunk at the same time. If you're agile, you might hug the tree using your arms and legs. I've also seen people hugging a tree by standing with their back in contact with the tree, and with their arms reaching behind them to hug the trunk. Alternatively, you might like to stroke the tree, or sit with your back resting against the trunk. You'll feel calmer and more relaxed after hugging a tree, and this increases your chances of attracting good luck.

Acorns have always been a symbol of good luck, and because oaks are long-living trees, carrying an acorn with you ensures you'll live a long life and always be young at heart.

Buckeyes or horse chestnuts are flat on one side and rounded on the other. They're called buckeyes as the circular mark on the flat side looks similar to the eye of a deer. They probably became a good luck charm because they're pleasant to hold and people decided to keep them. They're a popular good luck charm.

Interestingly, hairy caterpillars are said to be a sign of good luck. You need to pick the caterpillar up and toss it over your shoulder to activate the luck. Don't turn around to see where the caterpillar landed, as that reduces the amount of good luck you'll receive.

People have tossed coins into ponds, springs, wells, and fountains for thousands of years. As water is essential for life, anywhere where water appeared was considered holy. Tossing a coin was a gift to the spirits and gods who provided the clean water. While doing this, people prayed and asked the gods for prosperity and good luck. Today, it's considered a charming tradition, and people still make a wish. These wishes often come true, as the ritual of deciding on a wish and tossing the coin makes people focus on something specific, and consequently attracts good luck.

It's considered lucky to see a rainbow, as it symbolizes the bridge between the natural and supernatural worlds. However, in the United Kingdom it's considered bad luck to point at a rainbow. An ancient story says that there's a pot of gold at the end of the rainbow. Even if you can't get to the end of the rainbow, you'll gain good luck if you can see both ends of it simultaneously. Many people make a wish when they see a rainbow.

It's also thought to be a sign of good luck to find a feather, and the luck is doubled if the feather is black. Traditionally, you were supposed to pick it up and stick it into the ground. Nowadays, many people believe white feathers come from angels and are a sign of protection and good luck. Consequently, many people today keep white feathers as a good luck charm.

Ladybugs, or ladybirds as they're known in the United Kingdom, received their name in the Middle Ages when they were dedicated to the Virgin Mary and were known as the "beetle of our lady" (Vinci, 45). Seeing a ladybug is a sign of good luck, and it's even more fortunate if it lands on you. If it does, count the number of spots on its back. This indicates the number of lucky months you can look forward to. Allow the ladybug to fly away when it wants to. You'll lose all the good luck it provides if you force it to leave by brushing or blowing it off. It's extremely bad luck to kill a ladybug. Ladybug charms are often worn to attract good luck and prosperity.

Crickets have always been considered lucky; their chirping provides company as well as a warning of possible danger, as crickets stop chirping at the first sign of anything untoward. It's bad luck to kill a cricket. Charms in the shape of crickets are often worn to attract good luck and happiness.

Frogs have been considered lucky animals for at least two thousand years. Because of their noisy love-play, ancient Greeks considered them a symbol of fertility. The Roman philosopher and writer Pliny the Elder (23–79 CE) wrote that frog charms attracted friends and everlasting love. In Japan, frog charms are worn by travelers to ensure they return home safely. In China, the frog symbolizes a happy home and family life. In America, it's a sign of good luck if a frog comes into your home. You should also make a wish when you see your first frog in the spring.

In North America, seeing a robin flying upward is a sign of good luck. However, it's bad luck to see a robin flying downward. No matter which way it's flying, you should make a wish whenever you see a robin.

Crows are generally considered to be unlucky birds; even today, some people bow to avert bad luck when they see a single crow. However, two crows flying together is a sign of good luck. You should make a wish if you see a crow gliding through the air. Your wish will be granted if it doesn't flap its wings before disappearing from view. If it does flap its wings, you must turn away. If the crow has disappeared from view when you look back, there's a possibility that your wish may still come true.

Blue and red birds bring good luck. So do blackbirds, doves, ducks, hummingbirds, kingfishers, martins, peacocks, pigeons, storks, swallows, woodpeckers, and wrens. The humble sparrow is considered lucky in China and Indonesia, and all around the world it's considered bad luck to kill one.

How much luck an animal provides depends on where in the world you happen to be. In Germany, a pig is lucky. The scarab was a lucky symbol for the ancient Egyptians. In India, the elephant is sacred and lucky. Rabbits are considered lucky in some places, and many people around the world say, "white rabbits" or "rabbit, rabbit, rabbit" on the first day of the month to attract good luck. Dolphins are a sign of good luck in some countries, including Italy, Turkey, and the United States. Goldfish are considered lucky in many parts of the world.

There are a number of lucky animals in feng shui. These include the bat, crane, cricket, deer, dog, dragon, duck, elephant, frog, horse, koi (carp), monkey, ox (cow), phoenix, pig, rabbit, swan, tiger, and tortoise.

46

◆

Luck in Gemstones

Gemstones are usually sought after because of their beauty, but throughout history people have collected them for other reasons, such as good luck, as well. Gemstones have been found in prehistoric burial grounds, in the ruins of Sumerian cities, and in ancient Egyptian tombs. When the tomb of Tutankhamun, the boy king who ruled Egypt some thirty-three hundred years ago, was opened in 1922, it was packed with rings, bracelets, amulets, charms, diadems, collars, and breastplates made of gold and set with precious gems. Many scholars believe that ancient people originally wore gemstones as amulets and lucky charms, and wearing them for adornment was a later development. All crystals and gemstones contain energy and are believed to attract good luck to whoever owns them.

You can use gemstones in many ways to attract luck. You might display one or several on your desk. Every time you see them, they remind you how lucky you are. You can pick one up and fondle it whenever you feel the need for additional luck. You might turn a special gemstone into a ring, bracelet, brooch, or necklace. This enables you to wear it as a fashion accessory and attract good luck at the same time. You might carry a gemstone in your pocket or purse. Handling it will remind you how lucky you are.

Many people wear a gemstone that relates to their birth sign. Jewish people in eighteenth-century Poland are believed to be the first people to wear gemstones that related to the month in which they were born. (Kunz, 307) In 1912, the American National Retail Jewelers Association created a list of gemstones for each month that they hoped would satisfy everyone. In 1952, the Jewelry Industry Council in America came up with a slightly amended list that is still in use today:

- January: Garnet (constancy)

- February: Amethyst (sincerity)

- March: Aquamarine (foresight) or bloodstone (courage)

- April: Diamond (innocence)

- May: Emerald (happiness in love)

- June: Pearl (purity), moonstone (passion), or alex-andrite (luck)

- July: Ruby (purity)

- August: Peridot (beauty) or sardonyx (happy marriage)

- September: Sapphire (love)

- October: Opal (hope) or pink tourmaline (love)

- November: Topaz (fidelity) or citrine (clarity of thought)

- December: Turquoise (prosperity) or zircon (success)

Unfortunately, jewelers failed to realize that most people prefer to wear a stone that relates to their astrological sign rather than the month they were born in. Not surprisingly, experts have failed to agree on which stones relate to each sign. Here is a list of suggested lucky gemstones for each sign of the zodiac:

- Aries: Bloodstone, diamond, jasper, ruby

- Taurus: Sapphire, turquoise, emerald, lapis lazuli, carnelian

- Gemini: Agate, pearl, moonstone, alexandrite, citrine

- Cancer: Emerald, moonstone, ruby, olivine

- Leo: Agate, diamond, sardonyx, peridot

- Virgo: Jade, sapphire, carnelian, jasper

- Libra: Opal, lapis lazuli, tourmaline, emerald, aventurine, jade

- Scorpio: Beryl, aquamarine, topaz, citrine, garnet

- Sagittarius: Topaz, jacinth, peridot, turquoise, zircon

- Capricorn: Garnet, ruby, malachite, black onyx, jet

- Aquarius: Amethyst, garnet, malachite, turquoise, zircon

- Pisces: Aquamarine, bloodstone, amethyst

If you are particularly fond of the stones related to your sign, they would make good lucky charms. However, you aren't limited to just those, nor is there any reason to avoid any different stones that appeal to you. Here are some possibilities:

Agate

Agate is a variety of quartz available in a wide variety of colors, including white, gray, orange, blue, red, black, and banded (containing bands of different colors). It has been worn as jewelry since Babylonian times. It's considered lucky as it provides balance, strength, and protection.

Alexandrite

Alexandrite is an unusual stone as it is green in daylight but appears to be light red in artificial light. It gained its name as it was discovered on April 29, 1839, the twenty-first birthday of the heir to the throne of Russia, Alexander II. It's worn to attract both love and good luck.

Amazonite

Amazonite is a semiopaque blue-green crystal. It helps you set worthwhile goals and also provides the necessary motivation to achieve them.

Amethyst

Amethyst is a violet stone that provides good luck, intuition, spirituality, and wisdom. At one time it was known as the "bishop's stone," and rosaries made from it were said to enhance intuition and eliminate stress and tension.

Aquamarine

Aquamarine ranges in color from white to brilliant blue. It's a symbol of purity, and in many Asian countries is often given to brides on their wedding day. Aquamarine helps eliminate stress and worry. It also provides tranquility, peace of mind, happiness, and courage.

Aventurine

Aventurine is found in several colors, including yellow, green, blue, and red. It's considered to be a stone of chance and good luck. Consequently, it's a favorite stone of gamblers.

Carnelian

Carnelian is a reddish-brown gemstone that provides physical energy and is considered lucky for anyone involved in athletic pursuits. It also provides inner strength and a sense of humor. Napoleon had a carnelian attached to his watch chain.

Cat's-Eye

Cat's-eye is a gemstone that when cut in a convex form reveals a luminous band that looks like the eye of a cat. Cat's-eye has many uses. It helps you understand and accept others as they are. It enhances determination, persistence, and lofty goals. It also provides insight, protection, and good luck.

Citrine

Citrine is a yellow, orange, or gold member of the quartz family. It's considered lucky for anyone involved in business, and is sometimes known as the "merchant's stone" or the "money stone" because of its alleged ability to attract money. It enhances communication and decision-making.

Diamond

Diamond is a transparent form of pure carbon, and is considered the king of gems. It's a universal symbol of love. Diamonds also attract luck in all financial dealings.

Emerald

Emerald is a bright green beryl that has long been associated with Venus, the goddess of love. Consequently, emerald attracts love and good luck. It also eases troubled minds, and attracts prosperity.

Garnet

Garnet is usually red but can be found in many other colors. Garnets bolster confidence and provide good luck for people in business and those who are following a set career path. It's believed to change color when its owner is in danger.

Hematite

Hematite is usually steely gray but can also be black, brown, or brownish-red. It's sometimes known as "the stone that bleeds" as it gains a reddish streak when rubbed against a test surface. The name hematite comes from the Greek *haimatos*, which means "blood." It provides courage, motivation, and good luck in all close relationships.

Jade

Jade is a hard stone that varies in color from white to green. It enhances friendship, and is worn for protection, longevity, and good luck. In China, jade has been treasured for more than four thousand years.

Lodestone

Lodestone, also called magnetite, is magnetic iron ore. It's been considered lucky for at least four thousand years, and Alexander the Great issued lodestone to his soldiers as lucky charms. Women are not supposed to wear lodestone at any time, but men can wear it to attract strength, courage, virility, and good luck.

Malachite

Malachite is a copper ore that contains patterns of both light and dark green. Six thousand years ago, the ancient Egyptians mined malachite to create amulets and lucky charms. Malachite is sometimes called the "salesperson's stone" as it's said to provide salespeople with confidence, eloquence, protection, and the ability to sell. Today malachite is one of the most popular stones for lucky charms.

Moonstone

Moonstone is a form of feldspar. It gained its name from its luminous white and gentle blue colors, reminiscent of moonlight. It's sacred in India and is believed to bring good luck to anyone who wears it. It's said to arouse the passions, and is a popular stone for lovers, and people searching for love.

Quartz

Quartz is one of the most commonly found minerals around the world. It's available in many colors, but clear and rose quartz are the varieties used most often to attract good luck.

Red Jasper

Jasper is usually red, yellow, brown, or green. Red jasper provides courage and independence. It eases stress and provides strong protection. It's considered a lucky stone for anyone who performs in front of the public.

Ruby

Ruby has always been a popular stone. It attracts abundance, success, and eternal love. It's said that the more rubies you possess, the happier you'll be. You'll also have an abundance of good luck.

Sodalite

Sodalite is a royal blue gemstone that calms the nerves and provides inner peace. It's considered a lucky stone for people involved in any form of communication.

Tiger's-Eye

As tiger's-eye provides confidence and self-assurance, it's sometimes known as the stone of independence. It's always been used to attract good luck. Because of these associations, it's supposed to be especially useful for people with big aspirations.

Tourmaline

Tourmaline is sometimes known as the "gemstone of the rainbow" as it can be found in all the colors of the rainbow. Black tourmaline removes negativity and provides good luck and happiness. Green tourmaline attracts worldly success. Pink tourmaline attracts love and good friends. Tourmalines that contain two colors provide additional good luck when required.

Turquoise

Turquoise is the most popular stone in the world for good luck, and attracts happiness, love, and prosperity. It's often called the lucky stone and is also believed to remove any negativity that might affect its owner.

47

◆

Divination
and Dreams

Throughout history, people have used different methods to predict the future. Almost everyone wants to know if they'll enjoy love, luck, happiness, success, children, and good health in their future. They also want to know about the well-being of close friends and family. After this, they want to know about the future of their country, and the world. It's no wonder divination is as popular today as it ever has been.

Philosophers and theologians have always had difficulty with the concept of divination. After all, if the future could be foreseen, the implication is that it has somehow already taken place. Many years ago, I was told about a man who was looking out the window of a moving train. The countryside he saw was the present moment to this man. The train engineer could see this man's future, and someone looking out the window at the end of the rear carriage was able to see his past. In addition, someone standing on a nearby hill could see the man's past, present, and future all at once. Of course, the future is not preordained; we all possess free will and are consequently in charge of our own fates.

We all create our futures by our thoughts and actions. Everything we do creates energy that not only influences the present but also extends into the future. When I was in India in the 1960s, a holy man told me that when someone does a good deed, the universe expands. Similarly, when someone does a bad deed, the universe contracts. I know now that this is part of Hindu philosophy, but at the time I was impressed with the man's wisdom. (Vivekananda, 217)

You'd think that with our ability to create our own futures, there wouldn't be any need for different methods of divination to see what the future holds. However, this is certainly not the case, and people today are just as interested in finding out about their future as they have been at any other time in human history. Interestingly, many people want to find out about their future at least partly because they have the ability to change it if they're not happy with what they learn.

It can be helpful to have a reading from a good psychic reader if you have doubts, concerns, or serious questions about your future. The reader will tell you something about your past, present, and future. However, he or she can only tell you about the sort of future you're going to have if you continue living the same sort of life as you are now. Ideally, if you're not happy with what you learn, you'll take action and change your future. Even if a divination appears to be incorrect, you'll still learn some useful, relevant, and helpful information.

There are a number of so-called prophecies in the Bible that failed to eventuate. Did this mean the seer had failed or was fraudulent? No. The predicted future didn't occur because the people, having been warned, changed their behavior, and consequently their destiny.

Over the years, people have invented thousands of methods of divination. Some, such as entrail reading and sacrificing animals, have fortunately gone out of fashion. Others, almost as old, such as astrology and palmistry, are still popular today.

Arguably, the simplest method of divination is the pendulum. (See chapter 43, on the pendulum.) This provides yes and no answers to questions. Consequently, you can ask it questions such as: "Would it be a good move to do (whatever it happens to be)?" "Is good luck coming my way?" or "Should I ask my boss for a pay rise on Thursday?"

Dreaming is possibly the oldest method of divination, and the most famous precognitive dream of all is in the Bible. Pharaoh dreamt of seven fat and seven lean cows, and seven healthy ears of corn and seven thin ears of corn. Joseph successfully interpreted the dream for Pharaoh. The fat cows and the seven healthy ears of corn showed that Egypt would enjoy seven years of prosperity, and the seven thin cows and ears of corn showed it would be followed by seven years of famine (Genesis 41:1–40).

Most dreams relate to what is going on in your life and usually help sort out what you've experienced during the day. Everyone dreams, even people who think they don't—they simply don't remember them.

How to Remember Your Dreams

Some people find it easy to recall their dreams, while others lose the memories within seconds of waking. If you use an alarm clock to wake up, the chances are you'll jump out of bed and immediately forget your dream. You'll have better results if you try to recall your dreams when you wake up on the weekend or at any other time when you're able to wake up naturally.

1. Place pen and paper, or some form of recording device, beside your bed to record your dreams when you wake up.

2. As you go to bed, tell yourself that you'll enjoy pleasant dreams and will remember them when you wake up. You need to state this firmly, as you want the message to reach your subconscious mind. Repeat this message several times before you fall asleep.

3. When you wake up, keep your eyes closed and lie quietly, without changing your position and wait to see what dream memories come back to you. At first, you might receive fragments of a dream, a single word, a feeling, or maybe nothing at all. Repeat the first three steps regularly until you start recalling your dreams.

4. Record everything you can remember. Sometimes you'll be able to remember most or all of a dream, while at other times you might capture only a few moments. Don't analyze or evaluate anything while recording your dream. You can do that later. The important thing is to record everything you can recall as quickly as possible before the dream fades and disappears. Once you've done this, read or play it to ensure that you haven't accidentally left something out.

Precognitive Dreams

Dreams can also provide glimpses of the future, especially if you have an important decision to make or are at a crossroads in your life. These often contain useful insights that can help you make the right decision. Dreams can also indicate possible futures. If, for instance, you're thinking about changing your job or career, you might experience a number of dreams, each providing information about different possibilities. It's important to carefully evaluate these and decide which future seems most appealing. The other dreams weren't wasted, as they gave you a number of choices and helped you make a decision. They also gave you a glimpse of what might be, rather than what will be.

Once you gain experience working with your dreams, you'll be able to ask specific questions before you fall asleep. The best way to do this is to write your question down before going to bed. Evaluate your dreams carefully when you wake up, as the answer might be quite different from what you expect and could even appear in the form of symbols rather than a direct answer.

Scientists have studied precognitive dreams for many years. During the 1960s and '70s, researchers at the Maimonides Dream Laboratory in New York conducted numerous experiments into dreams that involved precognition and telepathy. One of their experiments involved having the dreamer dream of an image that wasn't selected until after he or she had been woken. A total of 15,360 trials were conducted with Malcolm Bessent, a young English psychic. He recorded 7,859 successes. The odds of that result happening by chance were approximately five hundred to one (Ullman and Krippner, 180).

Lucid Dreams

Lucid dreaming occurs when you become aware that you're dreaming, and are able to control the dream and take it wherever you wish it to go. Most people have experienced this at some time or another, but usually fail to take advantage of it. One good way to enter a lucid dream is to set your snooze button on your alarm to go off about thirty minutes before you normally wake up. Turn it off, and allow yourself to return to the dream you were having, and before you return fully to sleep, see if you can direct your dream to a scenario that is lucky for you. This could be a business opportunity, a chance to meet a special person, a situation where everything turns out exactly the way you want it, or anything else that represents good luck for you. When you wake up, record everything you can remember about the dream, and then take the necessary steps to make it happen.

Daydreams

You can control your daydreaming in the same way. Sit down comfortably, relax, and then start thinking about your future and how you want to live your life. As you want to experience an abundance of good luck in your future, allow your daydreams to be expansive and happy. It's usually best to think about one area of your life each time you do this. You might, for instance, in one daydream, think about where you want to live, and then, in other daydreams, think

about the type of home you'll be living in, the relationships you'll be having, your career or type of work you'll be
doing, hobbies and other interests, travel, health, or your
spiritual growth. Again, write down the key points of each
daydream, analyze them to make sure that this is what you
want, and then work on making them a reality.

48

◆

TAROT

Tarot is the most commonly used method of divination in the Western world. It is younger than most systems of divination. No one knows exactly when or where they were first created, but the earliest tarot cards we know about were documented in Ferrara, northern Italy, in 1422.

Most tarot decks today are divided into two parts: the major arcana and the minor arcana. The word *arcana* means "secrets" or "mysteries." The twenty-two cards in the major arcana relate to the major events in our lives. These include births, deaths, marriages, successes, and disasters. The fifty-six cards in the minor arcana indicate events that can be changed if you so desire. The minor arcana cards are divided into four suits: cups, wands, swords, and pentacles. These relate to the suits of hearts, clubs, spades, and diamonds in the regular deck of playing cards. Each suit contains fourteen cards: the ace to ten, followed by page, knight, queen, and king. Regular playing cards discarded the knight, and changed the page's name to jack.

The suit of cups relates to friendship, love, relationships, and the emotions. The wands relate to action, ambitions, and activities. The pentacles relate to work, money, career, security, and stability. They also relate to home, family, and possessions. The swords relate to overcoming conflicts and other problems, logic, and rational arguments/thoughts.

If you study the tarot, you'll be able to do readings for yourself as well as others. Initially, it would be a good idea to find a professional tarot reader and have a reading to learn more about what is going on in your life. In fact, most tarot readers became interested in the subject after having a tarot reading themselves. After having a reading, you may decide to study it, too. I vividly remember everything that happened on the day I had my first tarot reading; I consider it a very lucky day.

Even if you decide not to learn more about tarot, you can carry certain cards around with you to help attract good luck. Once you've chosen a particular card, keep it in a pocket or purse, and make sure that you look at it at least three times a day. Each time, look at it closely, as you'll gradually find more and more symbolism in the card. Think about why you chose this particular card, and thank it for attracting good luck to you. Kiss it or hold it between the palms of your hands for about ten seconds, before putting it away again. Following is a list of the fifteen most important cards for attracting good luck.

The Empress

The Empress card shows a pregnant woman sitting in a beautiful garden. She has pictures of pomegranates on her garment, symbols of fertility and fruitfulness. This card symbolizes creativity, abundance, and the birth of something new. This card provides good luck to people who have a strong desire to achieve something and make a success of their lives.

The Lovers

The Lovers card shows a couple standing before the archangel Raphael. This card usually relates to romantic love but can also symbolize unconditional love for a friend or relative. This card provides good luck in relationships and decision-making.

Wheel of Fortune

The Wheel of Fortune card is the only tarot card that doesn't have a figure of a person on it. It consists of a circle denoting the wheel of fortune. This is a card of chance. It's considered a lucky card that can indicate a surprise win or money from an unexpected source.

The Star

The Star card shows a nude woman kneeling with one foot in a pool of water (signifying intuition) and the other foot on the ground (symbolizing logic). She's pouring water from two jugs, one into the pool, symbolizing the subconscious, and the other onto the land, symbolizing the conscious. The Star is a card of hope which shows that good things are ahead, usually after a difficult time in the recent past. It provides good luck for people who know what they want to achieve.

The Sun

The Sun card shows a small child riding a white horse. They symbolize innocence, purity, and joy. Overhead, a benign sun radiates its gifts of life and abundance. This is one of the most positive cards in the entire deck and shows you have plenty of enthusiasm and energy, and should use it to start something new. It indicates good luck in relationships, creativity, and financial matters.

The World

The World card shows a woman dancing inside a laurel wreath. She's draped in a purple sash, and holds two wands. The World card is highly positive as it indicates success and accomplishment. The person who chooses to carry this card is likely to receive satisfaction and possible recognition for their achievements. The woman is looking back to the past, but her body is moving forward into the future, showing that she'll soon be starting a new cycle of life. This card provides good luck in all areas of life as long as the person who carries it is prepared to work hard to achieve it.

Ace of Pentacles

On this card, a hand offering a pentacle (coin) emerges from a cloud. The scene shows a garden with a path leading to mountains in the distance. This card helps you attract new opportunities that will provide good luck and material rewards. If you carry this card, you'll need to remain alert for potential opportunities and ideas that you can capitalize on.

Seven of Pentacles

The Seven of Pentacles shows a farmer looking at his crop. He's satisfied with his progress but needs to be patient. Problems may still arise, but as long as he keeps his eye firmly on his goal, he will succeed. This is a lucky card for people who are on the way to success but haven't achieved it yet.

Nine of Pentacles

The Nine of Pentacles shows a well-dressed woman standing in her luxurious garden. She has achieved success on her own terms, doing everything in her own way. She had a dream, that she achieved after a great deal of hard work. This is a lucky card for women.

King of Pentacles

The King of Pentacles card shows a wealthy man sitting on a throne. This is a lucky card for men who are willing to plan ahead, work hard, demonstrate leadership abilities, and ultimately receive the rewards of their hard work.

Ace of Cups

The Ace of Cups shows a large cup overflowing with water that falls into a large pool. The cup is held by a hand emerging from a cloud. A dove flies toward the cup providing blessings from heaven. This card symbolizes joy, love, and contentment, and blesses new and existing relationships. It indicates the start of a highly positive period in life and attracts happiness, abundance, and good luck.

Three of Cups

The Three of Cups shows three ladies dancing in a field. They each have a cup raised high in the air. This card symbolizes joy, happiness, and good fortune. It also shows that cooperation and communication with close friends can provide lucky opportunities.

Nine of Cups

The Nine of Cups card shows a successful man sitting outside enjoying the rewards of his labor. He has a smile on his face, and looks serene and contented. The Nine of Cups is known as the "wish card," and promises success to people who know what they want, and are willing to pay the price to achieve it. It also shows that whatever you put out into the world will come back. You need to make a wish (set a goal) and keep focused on it if you intend to use this card to attract good luck.

Ten of Cups

The Ten of Cups shows a happy couple admiring their beautiful farm while their children play beside them. This card symbolizes emotional fulfillment, contentment, and a happy home and family life. This card indicates the successful realization of a long-held dream. It provides good luck for people seeking a fulfilling, happy, and long-lasting relationship.

Six of Wands

The Six of Wands shows a man wearing a laurel crown of victory, riding a white horse through an admiring crowd. It symbolizes a well-deserved success that should be celebrated and enjoyed, as it's come after a great deal of effort. This card provides good luck in all material aspects of life.

49

◆

Lucky Numbers

People have believed in lucky numbers for thousands of years. All numbers can be lucky, but odd numbers have always been considered luckier than even numbers. William Shakespeare referred to this concept in *The Merry Wives of Windsor* (Act 5, scene 1): "This is the third time; I hope good luck lies in odd numbers." Lucky numbers are usually single-digit numbers. Twenty-six hundred years ago, Pythagoras said there were only nine numbers, as every other number is a multiple that can be reduced down to a single digit.

Your lucky number should have some sort of meaning for you. It might be something ephemeral, such as your house number, or the number on the back of your favorite athlete's jersey. More usually, though, a lucky number has a personal connection to the person's name or date of birth.

Day of Birth

You might decide to use the day of the month you were born. If you were born on the 9th day of the month, your lucky number would be 9. If you were born on the 26th, your lucky number could be 26 or 8 (as 2 + 6 = 8).

Full Date of Birth

According to numerologists, your lucky number is worked out by adding your month, day, and year of birth, and reducing the result down to a single digit. Here's an example for someone born on April 28, 1980. 4 + 28 + 1980 = 2012. 2 + 0 + 1 + 2 = 5. This person's lucky number is 5.

If you prefer, you might like to change your lucky number every year. You do this by adding your month and day of birth to the current year and reducing it down to a single digit. My friend, who was born on April 28, would use 1 as a lucky number in 2021, as 4 + 28 + 2021 = 2053. 2 + 0 + 5 + 3 = 10, and 1 + 0 = 1.

Success Number

You can also use what is known as your success number, which relates to the day of the month that you were born on:

If you were born on the 1st, 5th or 7th day of the month, your success number is 5. These days are the 1st, 5th, 7th, 10th, 14th, 16th, 19th, 23rd, 25th, or 28th of any month.

If you were born on the 2nd, 4th or 8th day of the month, your success number is 8. These days are the 2nd, 4th, 8th, 11th, 13th, 17th, 20th, 22nd, 26th, 29th, or 31st of any month.

If you were born on the 3rd, 6th or 9th day of the month, your success number is 6. These days are the 3rd, 6th, 9th, 12th, 15th, 18th, 21st, 24th, 27th, or 30th of any month.

Your Name

You can also create lucky numbers by turning the letters of your name into numbers using this chart:

1	2	3	4	5	6	7	8	9
A	B	C	D	E	F	G	H	I
J	K	L	M	N	O	P	Q	R
S	T	U	V	W	X	Y	Z	

Numerologists usually use the person's full name at birth when using this chart, and you can create your lucky numbers by using your full name at birth, or your full name now, if you've changed it for any reason, such as marriage. You can also create lucky numbers by using the first name only. However, for lucky numbers, the name the person is generally known by is the name most frequently used. If your first name is Margaret but everyone calls you Peggy, that's the name you should use. There are three ways to do this:

This uses all the letters of the name the person is known by. Most people know me as Richard Webster. The first two letters of my name (R and I) are both 9s. C is a 3, H is 8, and so on. This gives me: 9 + 9 + 3 + 8 + 1 + 9 + 4 for my first name, and 5 + 5 + 2 + 1 + 2 + 5 + 9 for my surname. The total of all of these is 72, and 7 + 2 = 9. I could use 9 as my lucky number.

This uses all the vowels in the person's name. I have an I, A, E and a second E in my name. They total 20, and as 2 + 0 = 2, I could also use 2 as a lucky number.

The third method uses all the consonants. The consonants in my name add up to 52. As 5 + 2 = 7, If I wanted to, I could use 7 as my lucky number.

This gives you a variety of numbers to choose from. Once you decide on the number you're going to use, test it for a few months to see if you consistently like the number, and if it's producing results. If you want to use it for gambling purposes, such as the lotto, you can use any sequence of numbers you wish, as long as when the total of all the numbers are added up and reduced to a single digit, the final answer is your lucky number.

Here's some information about the nine lucky numbers to help you choose the right number for you.

One

One is considered a lucky number, as it is indivisible, and remains the same when multiplied by itself. It symbolizes the sun, God, and the active principle of creation. It also represents the male principle, and everything masculine. It's considered to be an independent, enterprising, and ambitious number.

Two

Two is considered a lucky number as it symbolizes a couple. It also represents opposites, such as good and evil, love and hate, and life and death. Thousands of years ago, two symbolized the mother and everything feminine.

Three

Three is considered a lucky number as it symbolizes a couple and their baby. Twenty-six hundred years ago, Pythagoras considered three to be the perfect number, as it indicated life and the continuation of the species. Three is also the number of the Trinity. We give people "three cheers." The medium at Delphi in ancient Greece stood on a three-legged stool. People have bodies, souls, and spirits. They also have a past, present, and future. The expression "third time lucky" and "third time's the charm" came about because people tend to believe that success will come after two failed attempts. There are also three wishes, three cheers, and three strikes. No wonder so many people consider it to be their lucky number.

Four

Four is considered to be the luckiest even number. There are, for instance, four elements, four cardinal directions, four seasons, four gospels, and four evangelists. There are even four suits in a deck of tarot cards, and each suit contains four court cards. Four signifies hard work, and people with four as their lucky number have the potential to do well in their careers as long as they're prepared to work hard.

Five

Five is considered a lucky number for many reasons. It represents the center of all things. Most people have five fingers on each hand, and five toes on each foot. In ancient Egypt and Greece, the number five was inscribed on doorways to ward off evil spirits. A five-pointed star, called a pentagram, is still used by many people today as a symbol of protection.

Six

As there are six sides to a cube, six is considered the number of harmony and balance. The Star of David, a six-pointed star created by two overlapping triangles, was originally called the Shield of David, and was believed to protect people from negativity.

Six is considered to be a lucky number for people who are honest, but unlucky for people who prey on others.

Seven

Seven has always been considered a lucky number because it is unrelated to any of the other numbers from one to ten, and is indivisible. There are other reasons why it's considered lucky. God took seven days to create the world. There were seven "planets" in the ancient world (Mercury, Venus, Mars, Jupiter, Saturn, Moon, and Sun). There are seven seas, seven days in a week, seven virtues, seven ages of man, and there used to be seven wonders of the ancient world. In the Bible there are seven wise and seven foolish virgins. The Jewish menorah (candelabrum) has seven branches that symbolize the seven heavens. The lunar cycle is twenty-eight days, and the moon starts a new cycle every seven days.

The seventh son of a seventh son, and the seventh daughter of a seventh daughter, is said to be extremely lucky. If the sum of a person's full date of birth is divisible by seven, he or she will always be lucky. And it's said that when you're in "seventh heaven," you couldn't be happier.

Eight

Eight is a practical number that favors people who are willing to work hard to achieve their goals. Eight symbolizes man's resurrection. After the six days of creation and the seventh day of rest, the eighth day promises a better life in the world to come.

Traditionally, eight is said to be luckier for people over the age of fifty. If you choose eight as your lucky number, you're likely to become luckier the older you become.

Nine

Nine has always been considered a powerful lucky number. Nine is three times the sacred number three. It's also remarkable because no matter what number it is multiplied by, the sum of the digits in the total will always reduce down until they total nine.

Human pregnancy lasts for nine months, cats are said to have nine lives, and "a stitch in time saves nine." Extremely happy people are said to be on "cloud nine." A well-dressed person is said to be "dressed to the nines."

50

◆

POSITIVITY AND
SELF-ESTEEM

Positive people expect good things to happen. Consequently, they're alert for potential lucky opportunities that people with a more pessimistic outlook overlook, or fail to turn to their advantage. Positive people are willing to try something new, persist when something is more difficult than expected, and are less discouraged when matters don't work out the way they wanted. This means that positive people think and act in ways that encourage them to seek out lucky opportunities. It also means that they expect a good outcome in everything they do. When you have a positive attitude, most people you encounter will respond to your enthusiasm in the same way. This alone will provide you with plenty of opportunities.

The positive approach to life provides people with confidence and self-esteem. Both of these qualities play a vital role in determining how much good luck someone will receive. Self-esteem describes how much worth or value the person places on themselves. People with good self-esteem like themselves and accept themselves as they are. People with low self-esteem are overly critical of themselves and hold themselves back or are otherwise avoidant to prevent the pain of rejection.

People with good self-esteem expect good things such as luck to occur, while people with low self-esteem expect the opposite. It's hard to attract good luck when you have a negative attitude and are feeling bad about yourself.

Positive people attract other positive people, thereby creating powerful friendships, stimulating conversations, and opportunities for all to increase their luck. In fact, being surrounded by positive, enthusiastic, forward-looking people who always look on the bright side of life is itself a sign that good luck is on your side.

Fortunately, it's possible to build up your self-esteem and become more positive and luckier as a result.

1. Focus on your strengths. You have many positive attributes and qualities that you may overlook. People with low self-esteem focus on their weaknesses, which prevents them from seizing lucky opportunities.

2. Be kind to yourself. We all tend to be harder on ourselves than we ever would be to others. Take time out every day to nurture yourself in some way.

3. Think positive thoughts. Use affirmations or deliberately turn your thoughts around whenever you find yourself thinking negative thoughts. Do this gently. Remind yourself that your negative thoughts are only self-talk; you have the power to think any thoughts you wish. Constantly think of success rather than failure.

4. Spend as much time as you can with positive people. Not only will you enjoy the mental stimulation and happiness these people provide, you'll increase your self-esteem as a byproduct.

5. Stop comparing yourself to others. You are a perfect you. Other people might appear to be living charmed lives, but you have no idea what stresses, anxieties, and other problems they might be facing.

6. Do something worthwhile that makes you feel happy and proud. An excellent way to do this is to help people who are less fortunate than you or organizations in need. A good friend of mine gained confidence by donating time to an animal shelter.

7. Forgive others and yourself. Holding on to past hurts means you're constantly thinking negative

thoughts that demolish your self-esteem and make you feel like a victim. Forgive yourself, and remember that the past is gone. We've all done things that we regret, but it's time to let them go and move forward again.

There are also techniques to increase your positivity.

1. Stand erect with your shoulders back and your head held high. Raise your arms high in the air and then bring them down to shoulder height and stretch them out as wide as you can. Bring your arms down to your sides and take three deep breaths, telling yourself how positive and enthusiastic you feel.

2. Smile, even when you feel you have nothing to smile about. The act of smiling sends positive messages to your mind and makes you feel good.

3. Spend as much time as you can with positive people, and avoid negative people as much as possible. Positive people will build you up and make you feel good, while negative people do the opposite.

4. Make someone happy. You can do this in many ways. A phone call to a friend you haven't seen for a while will make him or her feel happy. Doing a small task or errand without being asked to do it will improve someone's day. A word or two of encouragement will increase the mood of someone

who needs it. Simply saying thank you can make someone's day. See how many compliments you can make in a single day. You'll be surprised how many opportunities you have to make people happy with a few well-chosen words.

5. Nurture yourself. Look after your physical body by exercising, eating good quality food, and getting enough sleep. Laugh as much as you can. Spend time with good friends. Do something kind to yourself every day, such as reading a good book, enjoying a leisurely bath, meditating, or spending time on a hobby. You should also reward yourself whenever you reach a worthwhile target or goal.

6. Keep a folder of all the positive letters, emails, cards, and other communications you receive from others. You might like to write down compliments and other positive comments that other people have said to you as well. Whenever you feel the need for some positive reinforcement, go through the file and read all the positive comments that people have made about you.

7. Listen to music that makes you feel happy. This might be something upbeat and positive, some favorite songs, or maybe a piece of music that brings back happy memories.

8. Start every day by thinking of at least three things you're grateful for. Follow this by telling yourself that you're an enthusiastic, positive, and confident person who makes the most of every day.

Everyone is born with unlimited potential, and everyone has equal worth. Treat everyone well. Be kind to yourself, and gradually let go of your negative thoughts and beliefs. Doing this will increase your self-esteem, build up your positivity levels, and enable you to lead a happy and fulfilled life. It will also turn you into a naturally lucky person.

CONCLUSION

Now it's up to you. Sitting in an armchair waiting for good luck to arrive won't achieve anything. It's all very well to invite good luck into your life, but you also need to be prepared and willing to act as soon as the right opportunity presents itself. The best way to create good luck is to maintain a positive attitude, keep busy, socialize, try new things, be proactive, and remain alert for any signs of luck. Creating your own opportunities and then capitalizing on them as much as you can will you bring you all the luck you desire.

Keep affirming that you are a lucky person until you believe it with every fiber of your being. You must also believe that you are entitled to your share of good luck, and be prepared to do whatever is necessary to achieve it. Think about what you want from life and constantly tell yourself that you deserve nothing but the best, as you're a lucky person and your future is going to be positive, successful, and happy.

You also need courage. There's a famous expression that says: "Fortune favors the brave." This means that you need courage to take the first step toward success. You must be willing to take calculated risks. More than two thousand years ago, the Roman poet Virgil wrote *Audaces Fortuna iuval*, an adage that says Fortuna, the goddess of luck, helps those who are willing to take action.

Your luck will increase if you use some of the ideas in this book. Don't try just one idea, though—experiment with as many as you can, and you'll soon notice how much luckier you are. Once you've become successful, you can "revel in your good fortune," as a friend of mine says often. He's able to say this as he's been extremely successful in both his business and personal life. He also frequently says, "I'm a lucky man." I've always thought his positive attitude played a large role in his success.

Success may not happen overnight, but it will happen if you create your own luck. You can use this good luck to further your career, attract the ideal partner, enjoy a wonderful home and family life, achieve your goals, and lead a happy, fulfilling life.

While writing this book, I met a man who keeps a good luck diary. Every day he writes down all the good things that have happened to him during the day. He says that his luck has steadily increased since doing this, as he's constantly looking out for lucky things to write about. As a bonus, if he's ever feeling downhearted, he can read some of the entries in his diary and realize what an incredibly lucky person he is.

Because he's always finding good luck, he's creating a wealth of good luck. When you think about it, you make your own luck. Luck is the result of the choices you make every day. I wish you great success.

BIBLIOGRAPHY AND SUGGESTED READING

Aczel, Amir D. *Chance: A Guide to Gambling, Love, the Stock Market & Just About Everything Else*. London: High Stakes, 2005.

Austin, James J. *Chase, Chance, & Creativity: The Lucky Art of Novelty*. New York: Columbia University Press, 1978.

Barker, Eric. *Barking Up the Wrong Tree: The Surprising Science Behind Why Everything You Know About Success Is (Mostly) Wrong*. New York: HarperCollins, 2017.

Benitez, Armando. *Sheer Superstition: Outmaneuvering Fate*. Charlottesville, VA: Hampton Roads Publishing Company, 2000.

Bethel, Sheila Murray. *A New Breed of Leader: 8 Leadership Qualities That Matter Most in the Real World. What*

Works, What Doesn't, and Why. New York: Berkley Books, 2009.

Bille, Matthew A., Erika Lishok, et al. *The First Space Race: Launching the World's First Satellites*. College Station, TX: Texas A&M University Press, 2004.

Bloom, Benjamin S. *Developing Talent in Young People*. New York: Ballantine, 1985.

Carnegie, Dale. *How to Win Friends and Influence People*. New York: Simon & Schuster, 1937.

Carr, A. H. Z. *How to Attract Good Luck*. New York: Simon & Schuster, 1952.

Chopra, Deepak. *The Ultimate Happiness Prescription: 7 Keys to Joy and Enlightenment*. New York: Harmony Books, 2009.

Conwell, Russell H. *Acres of Diamonds*. Philadelphia: John Y. Huber Company, 1890.

Copen, Bruce. *The Practical Pendulum*. Sussex, UK: Academic Publications, 1974.

Cowley, Malcom. "Mister Papa" *Life Magazine* 26, no. 2 (January 10, 1949): 90.

Crowley, Aleister. *Magic in Theory and Practice*. New York: Dover Publications, 1976. Originally published for subscribers by Paris, France: Lecram Press, 1929.

Damisch, Lysann, Barbara Stoberock, , and Thomas Mussweiler,. "Keep Your Fingers Crossed!: How Superstition Improves Performance," *Psychological Science* vol. 21, iss. 7, May 28, 2010: 1014–1020.

Darke, Peter R., and Freedman, Jonathan L. "The Belief in Good Luck Scale," *Journal of Research in Personality 31*, 1997: 486–511.

Darwin, Charles. *The Correspondence of Charles Darwin*, Volume 24, 1876. Cambridge, UK: Cambridge University Press, 2016.

Darwin, Francis. *The Life and Letters of Charles Darwin*, volume 1. New York: D. Appleton and Company, 1899.

Dickens, Mamie. *My Father as I Recall Him*. London: The Roxburghe Press, 1897.

Dickson, Paul. *"Murphy's Law": The Rules*. London: Arrow Books, 1981.

Dolnick, Barrie & Davidson, Anthony H. Luck: *Understanding Luck and Improving Your Odds*. New York: Harmony Books, 2007.

Dryden, John. *The Works of John Dryden: Now First Collected in Eighteen Volumes*. Originally published in 1808. Reprinted in 2008 by BiblioLife, Charleston, SC.

Einstein, Albert. *Einstein on Cosmic Religion and Other Opinions and Aphorisms.* Mineola, NY: Dover Publications, Inc., 2009. (Unabridged reprint of *Cosmic Religion and Other Opinions and Aphorisms.* New York: Covici-Friede, 1931.)

Ellis, Keith. *Thomas Edison: Genius of Electricity.* Hove, UK: Priory Press Limited, 1974.

Emmons, Robert A., and Michael E. McCullough. "Counting Blessings versus Burdens: An Experimental Investigation of Gratitude and Subjective Well-Being in Daily Life," *Journal of Personality and Social Psychology* 84.2, 2003: 377–389.

Emmons, R. A. and Hill, J. *Words of Gratitude for Mind, Body, and Soul.* Radnor, PA: Templeton Foundation Press, 2001.

Emmons, Robert A. and McCullough, Michael E. *The Psychology of Gratitude.* New York: Oxford University Press, 2004.

Emmons, R. A. *Thanks! How the New Science of Gratitude Can Make You Happier.* Boston: Houghton-Mifflin Company, 2007.

Emmons, Robert. *Gratitude Works! A Twenty-One Day Program for Creating Emotional Prosperity.* San Francisco: Jossey-Bass, 2013.

Frank, Robert H. *Success and Luck: Good Fortune and the Myth of Meritocracy*. Princeton, NJ: Princeton University Press, 2016.

Frankl, Victor. *Man's Search for Meaning*. Revised edition. New York: Pocket Books, Inc., 1997.

Frazier, Mondo. *The Secret Life of Barrack Hossein Obama*. New York: Threshold Editions, 2012.

Gale, Robert L. *A Henry Wadsworth Longfellow Companion*. Westport, CT: Greenwood Publishing Group, 2003.

Gillman. Steve. *Secrets of Lucky People: A Study of the Laws of Good Luck*. Parker, CO: Outskirts Press, 2008.

Gittelson, Bernard. *How to Make Your Own Luck*. New York: Warner Books, 1981.

Green, Walter. *This is the Moment! How One Man's Yearlong Journey Captured the Power of Extraordinary Gratitude*. Carlsbad, CA: Hay House, 2010.

Greer, Mary. *Women of the Golden Dawn: Rebels and Priestesses*. Rochester, VT: Park Street Press, 1995.

Gunther, Max. *Instant Millionaires: The Secrets of Overnight Success*. Petersfield, UK: Harriman House Ltd., 2011. Originally published 1973 by Playboy Press, Chicago.

———. *The Luck Factor: Why Some People Are Luckier Than Others and How You Can Become One of Them*. Petersfield,

UK: Harriman House Limited, 2009. Originally published 1977 by Macmillan and Company, New York.

Gunther, Max. *How to Get Lucky: 13 Techniques for Discovering and Taking Advantage of Life's Good Breaks*. Petersfield, UK: Harriman House, 2010. Originally published 1986 by Stein and Day, New York.

Hill, Napoleon. *Think and Grow Rich*. New York: Fawcett World Library, 1960. Originally published 1937 by The Ralston Society (Merriden, CT).

Isaacson, Walter. *Steve Jobs: The Exclusive Biography*. New York: Little, Brown & Company, 2011.

Jackson, Victoria, and Michael Yeaman. *The Power of Rare: A Blueprint for a Medical Revolution*. New York: Regan Arts, 2017.

Jahn, R. G., et al. "Correlations of Random Binary Sequences with Pre-stated Operator Intention: A Review of a 12-year Program." *Journal of Scientific Exploration* 11, no. 3: 345–367. Tiburon, CA: The Society for Scientific Exploration, 1997.

James, William. *The Will to Believe and Other Essays in Popular Philosophy*. New York: Longmans Green & Company, 1897.

Jones, Francis Arthur. *Thomas Alva Edison: Sixty Years of an Inventor's Life*. New York: Thomas Y. Crowell Company, 1908.

Kaplan, Janice, and Barnaby Marsh. *How Luck Happens: Using the Science of Luck to Transform Work, Love, and Life*. New York: Penguin Random House, 2018.

Kern, Ken. *Cracking the Study Code: 101 Tips and Techniques to Raise Your Grades and Test Scores . . . Now!* www.safeschoolproductions.com, 2018.

Kralik, John. *365 Thank Yous: The Year a Simple Act of Daily Gratitude Changed My Life*. New York: Hachette Books, 2010.

Kroc, Ray. *Grinding It Out: The Making of McDonald's*. Chicago: H. Regnery Company, 1977.

Kunz, George Frederick. *The Curious Lore of Precious Stones*. Philadelphia: J. B. Lippincott Company, 1913.

Maple, Eric. *Superstition and the Superstitious*. London: W. H. Allen & Company, 1971.

Martin, John Barlow. *Adlai Stevenson: The Man and the Statesman*. London: Victor Gollancz, 1952.

Maslow, Abraham. *The Maslow Business Reader*. Hoboken, NJ: John Wiley & Sons, Inc., 2000.

Morisano, Dominique, Jacob B. Hirsh, Jordan B. Peterson, Robert O. Pihl, and Bruce M. Shore. "Setting, Elaborating, and Reflecting on Personal Goals Improves Academic Performance." *The Journal of Applied Psychology* 95 (2010): 255–264. doi:10.1037/a0018478.

Nightingale, Earl. *This is Earl Nightingale*. Garden City, NY: Doubleday & Company, Inc., 1969.

Paine, Sheila. *Amulets: A World of Secret Powers, Charms and Magic*. London: Thames & Hudson, 2004.

Partridge, Eric. *Origins: A Short Etymological Dictionary of Modern English*. London: Routledge & Kegan Paul, 1958.

Peale, Norman Vincent. *The Power of Positive Thinking*. London: World's Work (1913), 1953.

Radin, Dean I. "Effects of Consciousness on the Fall of Dice: A Meta-Analysis." *Journal of Scientific Exploration* 5, no. 1: 61–83. Tiburon, CA: The Society for Scientific Exploration, 1991.

———. *Entangled Minds: Extrasensory Experiences in a Quantum Reality*. New York: Paraview Pocket Books, 2006.

Rasmusson, Christer. *Turn Your Vision into Reality*. Norderstedt, Germany: Books on Demand, 2015.

Richards, Steve. *Luck, Chance & Coincidence*. Wellingborough, UK: The Aquarian Press, 1985.

Roth, Charles B., and Alexander, Roy. *Secrets of Closing Sales*. Englewood Cliffs, NJ: Prentice Hall, 1997.

Sanghi, Ashwin. *13 Steps to Bloody Good Luck*. New Delhi, India: Westland Limited, 2014.

Segall, Grant. *John D. Rockefeller: Anointed with Oil*. Oxford, UK: Oxford University Press, 2001.

Seligman, Martin. *Learned Optimism: How to Change Your Mind and Your Life.* New York: Free Press, 1994.

Smith, Ed. *Luck: What it Means and Why it Matters*. London: Bloomsbury Publishing, 2012.

Starr, Karla. *Can You Learn to be Lucky? Why Some People Seem to Win More Often Than Others*. New York: Portfolio/Penguin, 2018.

Stulberg, Brad, and Steve Magness. *The Passion Paradox: A Guide to Going All In, Finding Success, and Discovering the Benefits of an Unbalance Life*. New York: Rodale, 2019.

Summers, Heather, and Anne Watson. *The Book of Luck: Brilliant Ideas for Creating Your Own Success and Making Life Go Your Way*. Chichester, UK: Capstone Publishing Limited, 2006.

Tharp, Twyla. *The Creative Habit: Learn It and Use It for Life*. New York: Simon & Schuster, 2003.

Ullman, Montague, Stanley Krippner, and Alan Vaughan. *Dream Telepathy: Experiments in Nocturnal ESP.* New York: Macmillan Publishing Company, Inc., 1973.

Vinci, Leo. *Talismans, Amulets and Charms*. London, UK: Regency Press, 1977.

Vivekananda, Swami. *The Complete Works of Swami Vivekananda*, volume 1. Kolkata, India: Advaita Ashrama, n.d.

Ware, Bronnie. *The Top Five Regrets of the Dying: A Life Transformed by the Dearly Departing*. London: Hay House, 2012.

Webster, Richard. *Amulets & Talismans for Beginners*. St. Paul, MN: Llewellyn Publications, 2004.

———. *Color Magic for Beginners*. St. Paul, MN: Llewellyn Publications, 2006.

———. *The Encyclopedia of Superstitions*. Woodbury, MN: Llewellyn Publications, 2008.

———. *Flower and Tree Magic*. Woodbury, MN: Llewellyn Publications, 2008.

———. *How to Use a Pendulum*. Woodbury, MN: Llewellyn Publications, 2020.

———. *365 Ways to Attract Good Luck*. Woodbury, MN: Llewellyn Publications, 2014.

Willey, Raymond C. *Modern Dowsing*. Cottonwood, TX: Esoteric Publications, 1975.

Williams, Tennessee. *A Streetcar Named Desire*. New York: Signet Books, 1951.

Wilson, John Albert. *The Culture of Ancient Egypt*. Chicago: University of Chicago Press, 1956.

Wiseman, Richard. *The Luck Factor: The Scientific Study of the Lucky Mind*. London: Century. 2002.

To Write to the Author

If you wish to contact the author or would like more information about this book, please write to the author in care of Llewellyn Worldwide Ltd. and we will forward your request. Both the author and the publisher appreciate hearing from you and learning of your enjoyment of this book and how it has helped you. Llewellyn Worldwide Ltd. cannot guarantee that every letter written to the author can be answered, but all will be forwarded. Please write to:

Richard Webster
⅌ Llewellyn Worldwide
2143 Wooddale Drive
Woodbury, MN 55125-2989

Please enclose a self-addressed stamped envelope for reply,
or $1.00 to cover costs. If outside the U.S.A., enclose
an international postal reply coupon.

Many of Llewellyn's authors have websites with additional information and resources. For more information, please visit our website at http://www.llewellyn.com.